# YOUR NEXT
# 40,000 HOURS

# YOUR NEXT 40,000 HOURS

## FALLING INTO AN ILLUMINATING SECOND CAREER

### ELAINE SIU

NEW DEGREE PRESS

YOUR NEXT 40,000 HOURS
*Falling into an Illuminating Second Career*

ISBN     978-1-63676-488-7   *Paperback*
         978-1-63730-399-3   *Kindle Ebook*
         978-1-63730-400-6   *Ebook*

見山是山，見水是水。
見山不是山，見水不是水。
見山還是山，見水還是水。

*"See mountains as mountains, and rivers as rivers;*
*See mountains are not mountains, and rivers are*
*not rivers;*
*See mountains once again as mountains,*
*and rivers once again as rivers."*

—ZEN MASTER CHINGYUAN WEIXIN

# Contents

---

*To Bunnie and my inner child, I love you.*

# INTRODUCTION

———

In the summer of 2014, I quit naked.

In Chinese, this phrase "quit naked" refers to quitting your job without having another offer on the table. The term implies being completely exposed and stripped of all forms of security, and ultimately, shame. Of course, naked can also signify utter boldness and vulnerability. Standing naked in a herd of corporate sheep in suits is giving mainstream society the middle finger. It was the most irresponsible thing I ever did in my life.

My life has revolved around work since I graduated from law school at the age of twenty-one. Since I crave approval, success is a nonnegotiable life goal. Anyone who's tried knows you don't accidentally land a job in an international law firm or investment bank. It takes years of meticulous staging. The reverse-engineering goes back to getting into the right primary school. The elite resume building starts there. And if you manage to be at the top of your class at least most of the time, prevent the coming-of-age distractions that may derail you, push yourself to the limit and then some more, you may join other crème de la crème who, as the Chinese saying goes, indeed win at the starting line.

I joined the workforce at the turn of the twenty-first century. It has gotten even more competitive over the years. If I were a teenager now, I'd be at the bottom of the pile. I was lucky, depending on how you look at it.

Within the first three years of working, I was already looking at a six-figure annual income. Sure, there are startup founders who take home millions in their twenties, but the proportion of startups that attain billion-dollar valuation is only around 1 percent (CB Insight, 2015). For those with a lower appetite for risk, the elite and employed route is a clear, guaranteed path to success.

My peers and I used to joke about our hourly rate not being that much higher than someone earning much less than we did. We consistently worked ninety-hour workweeks; I've lost count of how many holidays I spent in the office. Weekends, of course, meant nothing other than the supporting staff not being there. Most days, we hailed taxis home well past midnight and were grateful that at least we didn't pull an all-nighter.

The news stories about people dropping dead at their office desks and investment bankers getting hooked on hard drugs to sustain in their jobs are not exaggerations. There's no free lunch. I put in the hours and gave nothing but my best. We all did. But there is light at the end of the tunnel. Many of my peers are now partners in law firms or in the C-Suite of some banks or corporations. As you climb the ladder, you do gradually get a little more say over your time and boundaries; all in all, it's not a bad deal. It's a step-by-step guide to success as defined and acknowledged by society.

What's wrong with a controlled career plan, precisely executed, with clear causality to money and recognition? Nothing—except if you can't help but yearn for something more. Then what?

First, you resist.

"Resist that temptation to want more! Who do you think you are? Do the responsible thing!" the typical internal critic goes. But to some, that urge for something more simply becomes too strong to ignore or they get some big wake-up call like a health scare or a loved one passing away or an accident—something big enough for them to reexamine their life and go, "Fuck it." The fuck-it moment for me was actually the threat of being promoted. I knew if I took one more step up the corporate ladder, that would be it. I would never have the guts to give it all up and pursue something more meaningful.

You have the fuck-it moment and that's when things start to become interesting. Before you know it, you suddenly find yourself in a second phase of life, beyond building one's identity and survival.

## THE SEARCH FOR MEANING

Even if you're not on a ninety-hour workweek, work occupies most of our waking hours for our entire adult lives. On average, we spend about eighty thousand hours of our lifetimes at work, based on a forty-hour workweek, fifty weeks a year, for forty years. It shouldn't come as a surprise that most people try to find meaning in their jobs. To a large extent, our work determines whether we've had a meaningful life at all.

Based on a 2017 survey of over two thousand American professionals across twenty-six industries, the average employee says their line of work "is about half as meaningful as it could be" (BetterUp, 2017).

That's sad.

I know how that feels because that was exactly how I used to feel.

In the same study, nine out of ten career professionals told researchers they would sacrifice 23 percent of their future earnings—an average of $21,000 a year—for "work that is always meaningful." The unfortunate reality, however, is that even you're willing to earn less, it still doesn't guarantee you can find more meaningful work.

What is "meaningful" work, anyway? That's a profound question for each of us to figure out for ourselves. Unfortunately, while we all know what "conventional success" looks like, most of us aren't equipped to recognize our life purpose, let alone create a vocation that makes purpose the focal point.

In the first half of life, we are busy trying to look good to ourselves and others. Success, security, and containment are almost the only questions. Most of us would recognize these as the early stages in Maslow's hierarchy of needs. As Richard

Rohr wrote in *Falling Upward* (2011), "The very unfortunate result of this preoccupation with order, control, safety, pleasure, and certitude is that a high percentage of people never get to the contents of their own lives!"

## YOU NEED MEANING, AND THE WORLD NEEDS YOU

One common story has dominated the world for centuries. It infiltrates our classrooms, dinner tables, workplaces, and the media. From Henry Ford to *Shark Tank*'s Kevin O'Leary, the stories are essentially the same: self-worth and respect from others based on how much one has accumulated and achieved.

According to Rohr, we are a "'first-half-of-life culture' largely concerned about surviving successfully." From traditional education systems to personal development books and courses, we are fed with this first-half-of-life culture mostly about successful survival and nothing much beyond that.

But humanity is now facing a very different survival challenge. Scientists and environmentalists have known and warned us that climate change is no longer just a concept for a long time. Extreme weather conditions and natural disasters are already destroying lives and livelihoods. In 2020, the COVID-19 pandemic triggered an unprecedented shared awakening. It has pierced the illusion that our world's mainstream story of bigger, faster, and more is sustainable or even desirable.

The global public health crisis highlighted, among other things, the proximity of existential risks upon the human race, fundamental and systematic flaws, such as those in the food system that urgently require reinvention, and the disproportionate adverse impact on vulnerable communities when things turn bad. With social distancing, travel bans, and working from home creating a new normal, many have found the headspace to turn within and examine what they are doing with their lives. The pandemic has actually been the fuck-it moment for quite a few people I've interviewed who have since made the shift to a second career driven by an urge to fix the world's biggest problems.

As much as the world needs more people to rise to the challenge and use their vocational life to contribute to society in a more meaningful way, we also need meaningful jobs more than ever as we try to get through these tough times.

When artist and activist Cleo Wade reflected upon the notion of hope in her book, *Where to Begin* (2019), she wrote, "We **earn** our optimism. We **earn** our hope."

The pandemic marked the sixth year since I had quit naked. I tried to become a yogi hippie and a digital nomad and failed; I started my own business and failed twice. I have been in and out of so many rabbit holes in search of "purpose," and I could not be more grateful that by 2020, I have already founded and was heading the Good Food Institute Asia Pacific, part of a global nonprofit that focuses on shifting the world away from industrial animal agriculture.

As the world came to a halt, the alternative protein sector I worked in experienced expedited growth and interest. The breakdown of food supply chains and outbreaks among workers in meat and poultry processing facilities shone a spotlight on the fundamental defects in our broken food system.

When the pandemic first started, I felt stressed, bitter, powerless, and overwhelmed like many others as the situation spun out of control and affected every aspect of our lives. I eventually chose to feel empowered because of the dedication to my vocational life. Every day, through the work I chose to do, I was creating solutions to some of the world's most pressing problems. I *earned* my optimism and I *earned* my hope. It really felt like I had the best job in the world when this was the message I could give to my team through the crisis:

"I was extremely inspired when I read through our monthly report. It reminds me of why we're doing what we're doing, the brilliant minds that we're working with, and the potential impact we can make together. At a time like this, every one of us can take our power back by being part of the solution. We **earn** our optimism, we **earn** our hope, from the choices we make and the actions we take."

### AN ILLUMINATING SUBSISTENCE

While the bad news is that we are living in a pivotal moment when there are a lot of problems—existential problems like climate change, which we need to solve in our lifetime—the good news is that there is no shortage of truly meaningful work out there. In fact, much of this work is desperately in need of someone to do it!

During this period of change, there are two realities we can choose to spend our lives in: the reality of achievement and the reality of true progress. Today, many people's focus is shifting to doing good and leaving the world a better place. This can include being successful, but it also encompasses so much more beyond that.

It is from personal experience I'm saying this to you. It's possible to create a life you love, one that allows you to devote your time and energy toward what you truly believe in, to progress in life in a meaningful way, and to make the impact you're meant to make in the world. And a huge part of that is creating a vocational life that is truly an illuminating subsistence.

But how?

The three parts of the book will take you through the three stages of the path to self-actualization: dissolution, evolution, and transcendence. As ninth-century Zen Master Qingyuan Weixin's teaching goes, at the first stage, we see mountains as just mountains (Watts, 1951). We conform to the basics and norms, we build our identity, and we climb the societal ladder. These are the things we learn to dissolve in order to take our beings to the next level. Dissolution can be the most challenging phase if you're a mid-career professional like I was. Quitting your "successful" first career requires nothing less than a spiritual transformation. Dissolution can also be the most liberating part of the journey where you unlearn everything that no longer serves you and return to your truth.

At the second stage, we see mountains are not really mountains. We begin to question beyond the form, beyond the obvious. Through growing pains, we evolve. I will share with you the misunderstandings I had about this "purpose" I was so desperate to find. The misguided projection of my purpose led me down many detours, including becoming an entrepreneur, a hippie, and many other things from my chronicle of failures. Most of the stories of how to do it right are from people I've had the honor of knowing or working with.

Since we all work eighty thousand hours on average in our lifetimes, I'm calling this second career phase "Your Next 40,000 Hours." Some people only start searching for more mid-career, some realized it in a few years into their first jobs, and some never get there. I will introduce the theory of effective altruism to provide you with some much-needed structure and definition and examples of purpose-driven, high-impact careers others have launched.

And finally, at the third stage, we seek to transcend. We go full circle to see mountains once again as mountains but with an elevated understanding and perspective. This third phase is post-launching your second career. You think you're still climbing *up* the career ladder? Spoiler alert: you're in for a magnificent fall into the deep end where enlightenment is promised. This is what Richard Rohr calls "falling upward."

I've not reached the "promised land," so all I can tell you is I intuitively know it's there. I've had a glimpse of others who are closer to it than I am, those who seem to be falling with a little more grace than I have. You're embarking on an enchanted journey. There is still darkness in the second half of life, but even at its darkest moments—as I've been through quite a few of them—I can assure you that you're still more elevated and illuminated than you ever have been.

## LIVE A BIGGER LIFE

You may have lived your life so far following the conventional script: get good grades at school, work a well-paid job, climb the corporate ladder, buy and own more stuff. If after achieving all that, you find yourself unfulfilled and feeling empty inside, you're probably one of us weirdos who want more out of life.

Maybe you thought this kind of life was only for the fortunate few, so you settled for a vocational life that seems reasonably successful on the outside but highly unfulfilling within. Most of us are just too afraid to choose the path less travelled, to want something beyond what most people strive for, and to unleash a life sweeter than success, but the longer you settle, the more stuck, frustrated, and even miserable you become.

Nothing is more heart-wrenching than seeing enormous amounts of wasted talent and souls that can better in the world stuck living tiny lives just because they don't know where to start—or restart.

I started writing this book with mid-career professionals in mind for two reasons. First, this was my personal journey; second, I was frustrated with how difficult it was to hire the right people when I was building a nonprofit startup that worked on disrupting the meat industry. For the type of work we did, I needed to hire people who could bring in a lot of career assets like subject matter expertise, industry experience, and a network, and hit the ground running.

It's not easy, especially in Asia, to convince a biotech scientist, a food industry veteran, or a high-level marketing executive to join a nonprofit when they have a stable and lucrative career going within Big Pharma or Big Meat. I thought the struggle was unique to mid-careerists who have high opportunity costs, but in the midst of writing this book and interviewing more people earlier in their career paths who have pursued second-phase-of-life work, I'm now convinced this story is more universal than I had assumed.

## WHY IT'S WORTH IT

It's not a walk in the park. Nope, it's going to be damn hard.

There, that's the truth. It will break you down and bring you to your knees; you'll shed tears of both joy and devastation—like love, birth, and death, anything else in life that pushes you to grow. It's as painful as the caterpillar radically transforming its body, breaking through and emerging as the butterfly. If you want it, it's worth it. If you're currently suffocating, it's worth it. If you have what it takes to leave this world a better place and be a better person, it's worth it.

Renowned environmentalist and scholar David Orr has said, "The plain fact is that the planet does not need more successful people. But it does desperately need more peacemakers, healers, restorers, storytellers, and lovers of every kind. It needs people who live well in their places. It needs people of moral courage willing to join the fight to make the world habitable and humane. And these qualities have little to do with success as we have defined it." If this resonates with you, you're ready to become more.

It really can take years to gradually shed the past, those extra layers, to let go of all sorts of conditioning and baggage, before one can be ready to make that life-transforming change. The clock is ticking; there's no time to waste. If you long for the freedom and fulfilment that comes with having a purposeful, altruistic, and impactful career, and you know you deserve the natural flow of love and energy that will manifest when you finally become who you're meant to be, I truly believe we all have the potential—and even the skills, talents, resources, whatever—to get us to the other side.

You already have the answer in you. Now let's surrender to your true path and illuminate your life and the world with your next forty thousand hours.

# PART I

# DISSOLUTION

## CHAPTER 1

# THE RABBIT HOLE OF FINDING PURPOSE

———

*"He who has a **why** to live for can bear with almost any **how**."*

—NIETZSCHE

It was at age twenty-six I started feeling that utter nothingness about life.

I looked fine on the outside. To be fair, I looked more than fine to others. I worked at a global law firm, my clients were listed companies and investment banks, and my boyfriend was in private equity. I was on a clear trajectory of the standard lifestyle supported by a high income and a respectable profession. I had just purchased my first investment property. I regularly recharged myself from my ninety-hour workweeks through amazing getaways whenever I got a week or two off between deals: sunset in Santorini, wandering in the

Old Medina in Casablanca, architecture walks to appreciate Gaudi's genius in Barcelona, and my next destination, Iceland.

I couldn't afford to fly business class on holidays yet, but all things considered, life was good. Or at least I *should* have felt it was good.

I couldn't figure out why I developed profound disinterest about everything that *should* have gotten me excited. I was obsessed with success, and I had worked very hard to position myself on the right path. I *should* have been quite pleased with myself. Instead, I was numb.

I didn't care. Don't get me wrong, I cared a lot about executing my job with excellence and being applauded by how great I was at what I did. But as for what I was actually helping to create in the world? Sure, we got this company listed and raised millions of dollars, and that company acquired for millions of dollars. Big deal (pun intended). I didn't care. Work is work. I found money and status in it, not meaning. Surely that's okay, and that's how people live.

A friend floated the idea of depression as a possible explanation. I dismissed it, as I thought depression should be about crying and being sad all day long. How ignorant I was. My life primarily revolved around work, and that's the case for most of us if we spend anywhere from eight to twelve hours a day working. I told myself that one day, if I couldn't get myself out of bed to go to work, that would be the day I'd deem this "condition" as prohibitive to my "normal functioning" and I'd seek help.

Surprise, surprise, soon enough I struggled to pull myself out of bed. I was not sad. I was numb, emotionally, and it was finally affecting me physically. That day, I exhausted all my willpower to fight against my lifeless limbs. I couldn't get to work. *Damn it, so now I really have to deal with this*, I thought. I was quite certain the psychiatrist would give me a different diagnosis because I looked way too good on the outside to be depressed.

"This is a classic case of depression," said Dr. Whoever.

"What?" I gasped. "So what do we do now? How long will it take to fix me?" Because, naturally, I had more important and urgent things to attend to.

As it turned out, Dr. Whoever wasn't able to fix me. Depression became the teacher in my life that pushed me toward a more fulfilling path.

### THE TEASE OF LIFE PURPOSE

Just to be clear, this book is not about depression. Whatever clinical term or categorization used, depression does not manifest identically across different individuals.

Let's expand our vocabulary here. You don't need to be labelled as "depressed" to want to find your life's purpose. My theory (and experience) is that you are likely to suffer some form of emotional or psychological distress if you keep denying your natural instinct to find and live your purpose. The onset of that internal struggle can happen very differently for each individual, including how long it takes for that itch to turn into a powerful urge and finally a must-do-something-about-it calling.

To me, the significance of depression is that it prompted me to find my purpose in life.

"But I simply don't know what my 'purpose' is!" you may say. Most of us don't. The burden of finding *that* purpose in itself can be very distressing. Furthermore, creating a career aligned with a life purpose unbeknown to you is even more daunting. How do you do it?

It has to be said at the outset that there is no universal formula for finding your purpose. In the beginning of my journey into this rabbit hole, the articles I read, the aptitude tests I did, and the workshops and trainings I completed all seemed to be some derivative of the Hedgehog Concept.

The Hedgehog Concept was developed by Jim Collins in his book *Good to Great* (2001). In Collins's own words, the Hedgehog Concept is "a simple, crystalline concept that flows from deep understanding about the intersection of three circles":

Circle 1. What are you deeply passionate about?

Circle 2. What can you be the best in the world at?

Circle 3. What drives your economic engine?

Collins named it the Hedgehog Concept based upon an ancient Greek parable that "the fox knows many things, but the hedgehog knows one big thing." It's important to note, though, that Collins was primarily writing this in the context of *business*. The idea guides a company to understand which "one big thing" it should be doing.

But wait, doesn't that sound familiar? Think back to how your career guidance counselor helped you figure out what to major in at university. There were three very similar questions: what are you interested in, what are you good at, and well, let's be practical, what can land you a paying job? It's the same trio of passion, competence, and money.

We all intrinsically know this magic trio and have been applying it in every decision we make with regards to the question "What should I do with my life?" albeit with different levels of success. Over time, most of us compromise or neglect our passion in exchange for a job we are reasonably good at and for which we get reasonably paid.

Collins says, "When all the pieces come together not only does your work move toward greatness but so does your life. For, in the end, it is impossible to have a great life unless it is a meaningful life. And it is very difficult to have a meaningful life without meaningful work." There it is: the promise of purpose; the aspiration to find meaningful work and eventually live a purposeful, fulfilling life. So for the longest time I was desperately trying to find out what I was deeply passionate about and whether it was possible to incorporate that into the work I was good at and would be paid for.

But something else was missing.

There is a fourth element to this.

If you google "life purpose," I bet you will find the Japanese term *ikigai* on the first page of the search results. It wasn't the case years ago when I first started searching for my life purpose, but now it is.

*Ikigai* is a term traced as far back as the fourteenth century, but it gained mainstream popularity at the turn of the twenty-first century as multiple researchers and authors reexamined and reinterpreted the concept from different angles. *Ikigai* is now commonly associated with studies of longevity, happiness, and yes, life purpose. Noriyuki Nakanishi of the Osaka University Medical School wrote that "[n]eeds associated with *ikigai* are not simply equal to the desires for biological satisfaction or the desires of humans as social creatures. They are individual desires of humans as spiritual beings" (Nakanishi, 1999).

The many interpretations of *ikigai* come down to one common theme: your reason for being (living).

In 2014, Marc Winn combined *ikigai* with other Western theories around finding life purpose. His simple, modern reading of *ikigai* went viral and is likely to pop up in your google search result for *ikigai* (Winn, 2014). That's where I found that fourth element I had been missing.

Winn interpreted *ikigai* as the intersection of four circles:

Circle 1. That which you love

Circle 2. That which you are good at

Circle 3. That which you can be paid for

Circle 4. That which the world needs

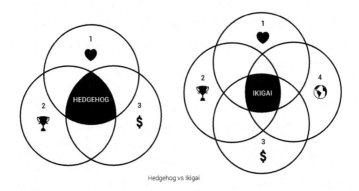

Hedgehog vs Ikigai

Comparing the Hedgehog Concept and *ikigai*:

Circle 1: "What you are deeply passionate about" is similar to "that which you love"; this one is about *passion*.

Circle 2: "What can you be the best in the world at" is similar to "that which you are good at"; this one is about *talent*.

Circle 3: "What drives your economic engine" is similar to "that which you can be paid for"; this one is about money, or in a broader sense, the *market*.

The most obvious difference is the additional Circle 4 in *ikigai*. "That which the world needs" is clearly a pursuit beyond understanding oneself and beyond self-interest. Note it's the only circle without the word "you" in it. That turned out to be the missing piece to my puzzle—what I'd call *mission*.

Over the years, Collins has expanded the Hedgehog Concept from business to the personal level. He applied the same three-circle structure of what I would similarly summarize as passion, talent, and market. But in 2010, Collins spoke about Circle 3 a little differently, mentioning the creation of not only economic value but also social value (The Drucker Institute, 2010).

Maybe "that which you can be paid for" and "that which the world needs" can be baked into one circle of "what drives your economic engine *and* creates social value." However, this is exactly where it gets interesting. Can they fit in the same circle? Or are they potentially in conflict, at least sometimes?

What has economic value is determined by market forces. Something's economic value is essentially what someone is willing to pay for it. If you are currently paid to do a job, no matter what that job is, it has intrinsic economic value; the hard proof is that you're paid to do it.

Just because something has economic value does not necessarily mean the world needs it. Some people in the world *want* it, that's for sure, because they are willing to pay for it. It doesn't translate that this thing some people in the world *want* has any net positive value to the world—considering other stakeholders beyond the buyer—for example, other people, other species, and the environment.

This distinction is key to me in finding my purpose in life and the core of what the second phase of life is all about.

The intersection of four circles: Passion, Mission, Talent, Market (**P-M-T-M**) is how I want to build my second career to resemble.

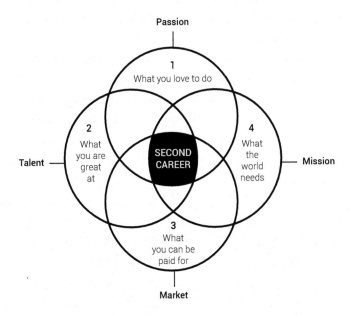

## THE "NO SUCH JOB" DILEMMA

But this intersection of P-M-T-M, is it real? Does it exist?

Christopher Michaelson, assistant professor of ethics and business law at the University of St. Thomas in Minneapolis, Minnesota, conducted a classroom exercise over several years. He asked business school students these three questions:

1. *A year out of this program, what do you expect your job will be?*

Michaelson described this as "the pragmatic question of market fit, the near-term reality that loans need to be repaid, foundations built, and families supported." This is what I call the Talent-Market (Circle 2 plus 3) combo, or the default job. Most of us are in jobs of this nature.

2. *What kind of job contributes the most to general well-being?*

This points to the creation of social value beyond self-interest and economic necessity for basic survival. This is Mission (Circle 4).

3. *Practicality aside, if you could be doing anything ten years from now, what would it be?*

In other words, if money is not an issue, if the sky is the limit, what is your dream job? This is Passion (Circle 1).

The result? There was almost no overlap among students' answers to these questions.

For the first question, students responded with generic corporate functions such as finance, marketing, and information technology—no surprise there. The second question relates to the other end of the spectrum: what students deemed socially responsible. The answers included social worker, research scientist, and doctor. And third, the arts, entertainment, and sports were heavily represented in the dream jobs.

If we indeed believe that life's purpose lies at an *intersection*—of your passion, your talent, how you can make a living, and what the world needs—then Michaelson's students as good as believed they were not to find their life's purposes in their work. There was no overlap in their answers to these questions.

A few years ago, I would have given the same answers. My job was one thing: what I thought would contribute most to society was something else and what I would love to do—yet another list. My answers had no overlap when I applied for university, when I applied for my first job, and when I applied for my second, third, and fourth jobs. I was taught to accept that it was unrealistic to expect I could ever find a job where passion, mission, talent, and market intersect. And for more than a decade, I accepted that as a rule of life.

## WHY DO YOU NOT KILL YOURSELF?
I had to reexamine this acceptance when my therapist advised that one of the major root causes of my depression was what I did for a living.

"Your career choice is creating too much inner conflict for you. You may want to consider changing your work," she said.

"If I stop lawyering, where am I gonna find the money to pay you?" I didn't say that out loud.

In hindsight, if I had done logotherapy, maybe I would have saved a few years searching for my answer.

Viktor Frankl, professor of neurology and psychiatry at the University of Vienna Medical School, distinguished his school of psychology (logotherapy) from traditional psychoanalysis. In psychoanalysis, the patient tells the therapist things sometimes hard to say; in logotherapy, the patient has to listen to things that are sometimes hard to hear (García and Miralles, 2017).

I like this guy already. After years of psychoanalysis and therapy, I got so bored of talking about my stuff. I remember I finally stopped going to therapy after saying to my psychologist, "I'm so sick of talking about myself. Maybe you can tell me something about you instead?"

One of Frankl's first questions to his patients was typically, "Why do you not commit suicide?" Straight to the point—love that.

It echoes with *ikigai*. Logotherapy is about finding a reason to live.

It didn't help me much to look into the past and analyze my neurosis. I'd rather look toward the future. In that future, the promise needs to be more than happiness (pleasure) and what can really create a sufficient reason to live is having a life purpose (meaning).

Many people get stuck in the first phase of life where basic survival instincts govern all. The career goal focuses on building up an identity accepted by society and earning enough to provide for oneself and one's family. But some face another survival crisis, and that's the rise of existential frustration: an emptiness stemming from the lack of or a skewed life purpose that can become a black hole sucking up a person's will to live.

What is refreshing about logotherapy is it does not see this frustration as mental illness, but rather as spiritual anguish. It is not a symptom of something wrong. It is perceived from a different perspective as a catalyst for change. As I—and many other like-minded people out there, I'm sure—were driven to seek a "cure" for what we were suffering from, we embarked upon a new journey that is the second phase of life.

Frankl went even further to say our health depends on the natural tension that comes from comparing what we've accomplished so far with what we'd like to achieve in the future (Frankl, 2006).

That's consistent with the creative tension I worked through to build up my second career. Discovering my purpose in life was my way of attempting to fill that existential void.

## THE FIRST VERSUS SECOND PHASE OF LIFE

My search for a life purpose led me into the second phase of life. In particular, the manifestation of a mission-driven second phase of life through the work I do.

In this phase you will find yourself longing to create a second career beyond just a job, occupation, or profession. You yearn for work that feels like a calling. At this stage, our drives are more selfless instead of self-interest oriented. It is that fourth circle of the *ikigai* diagram ("that which the world needs")—what I call Mission—we want to bring to the light.

The standard answer to "what is meaningful work?" seems to be something along the lines of "work that makes a difference and impacts society." Unfortunately, too many people use the catchphrase "make a difference" in anything and everything. More often than not, it is a completely empty claim.

I've made enough detours in this journey only to find out that when people say they want to change their career to "make a difference," they mostly mean making a difference in their own lives: "creating work on my own terms," "being my own boss," and "being a freedom-preneur" are a few common threads this phrase boils down to. It took me some years to realize how loosely many people define "meaningful work," which is often too self-serving for my taste.

The first phase of life is about the self and the second is beyond the self.

This isn't about a midlife crisis. According to Richard Rohr in *Falling Upward* (2011), "Second half of life is not strictly chronological. Some young people are already there, while many old folks are still in the first half of their lives, spiritually." And I have met a fair amount of young people who are already in their second half of life to know this is true. And yes, that gives me hope that maybe our world is not completely doomed after all.

But there is also no need to feel shame about the years you spent climbing the first career ladder. We need to form an identity and accumulate some basic safety and security to get started as individuals in society. We need some positive feedback and success early in life to build up our confidence and have a bit of what Rohr calls a "narcissistic fix" so we don't spend the rest of our lives trying to fill that void.

Paradoxically, you need to first build an ego to then have an ego to let go of and move beyond.

It is important to note that finding our purpose is likely a lifelong pursuit. It doesn't happen in an instant. It will evolve. It doesn't stop evolving because you don't stop growing as time passes and circumstances change. It is not a static concept or goal to achieve.

I sometimes still feel like I'm in the rabbit hole of finding purpose, but after all these years of learning through trial and error, it now feels less like descending into a black hole. The search for a life purpose has led me to a path less travelled, and borrowing Rohr's words, it feels like falling upward.

## CHAPTER 2

# BEEP, SNOOZE...BANG!

———

*"The ego is not who you really are. The ego is your self-image; it is your social mask; it is the role that you are playing. Your social mask thrives on approval. It wants control, and it is sustained by power, because it lives in fear."*

—DEEPAK CHOPRA

"I'm very grateful for having gone through three ICU operations in six days. I was very lucky that I woke up and fully recovered; and I woke up all right. It was a wake-up call."

It was 1995. Albert Tseng was in his third year majoring in mechanical engineering at the University of Waterloo in Canada. Growing up as a Chinese kid in Canada, Albert said he "took three maths and three science classes in high school; they call it the Chinese six pack." Albert laughed at what seemed like a lifetime ago. The path was clear: be a lawyer or doctor or engineer; Mum and Dad should be relieved.

After graduating from a prestigious school with a practical degree, Albert was on track to climb the ladder and buy a house in the suburbs. He was already interning every summer in the automotive industry. "I was part of strategic purchasing, which is basically hammering the suppliers to take ten cents out of a part that we put into a car." Well, at least he had a job.

But then Albert went to play basketball, fell, and cut his knee open. "I went to the hospital and got it stitched, but then overnight, I developed a high fever and was admitted to the hospital again; they started drawing lines of infection on my leg, and by the morning, it was up to my hip," Albert recalled.

Albert contracted an extremely rare flesh-eating bacteria called Group A strep necrotizing fasciitis (APIC, 2021). He was told that four people in Canada had it. Two of them died; one famous politician lost his entire leg. In that same year, Albert lost a friend of the same age to meningitis, and both of his grandfathers passed away. It felt nothing less than a miracle that Albert didn't lose his life. He didn't even lose a limb.

It was hard not to question everything, especially after dodging a bullet like that.

"1995 was like this crazy year of personal reckoning," said Albert.

### IT'S OKAY TO CLICK THE SNOOZE BUTTON

I'm by no means saying to look for a sign *that* big.

The universe doesn't always speak to you via flesh-eating bacteria, a dramatic accident, or someone close to you dying. While the universe can't wake you if you're pretending to be asleep, it's okay to click the snooze button after you received your wake-up call.

In fact, most of us do. I haven't been able to find any person through my journey and research who hasn't snoozed for quite a while after they got their first wake-up call—not even one. The average snooze period, based on my absolutely unscientific research methodology, is about seven years. That's the magic number.

So all I'm saying is, don't feel bad. You're good.

In Albert's case, after the accident, he pivoted from mechanical engineering to biomedical engineering. Having had a first-hand experience of the healthcare system, Albert saw a lot of problems technology could solve; technology being used in the automotive sector and in finance but not in healthcare.

Then Albert spent ten years building a stable career in healthcare. In each of those ten years, Albert travelled with his wife to a developing country for their anniversary—Africa, Latin America, the Middle East—to learn about the social issues happening globally. As the Chinese kid from Canada got more in tune with the bigger issues, working in healthcare in developed countries seemed less impactful. It was better than the automotive industry, but he realized there were many more important challenges in the world to tackle.

That's when Albert crossed the threshold. He and his family moved to South Africa to work on HIV healthcare systems. South Africa was, and still is, the epicenter of the AIDS epidemic in the world; 20 percent of all people living with HIV are in South Africa, and 20 percent of new HIV infections occur there too (Allinder and Fleischman, 2019).

"I probably have never been in an organization that it was so clear to me every day that we could change the world with the work we do; we can save lives," Albert recalled. "It's like if we could just get the cost of this treatment down by 10 percent, then we could put 10 percent more people on treatment next month. Six million people in South Africa were not on HIV drugs yet. It's basically a death sentence."

What came next for Albert may help us understand the importance of snoozing. You need time to build up knowledge and resilience, and to have the ability to deal with the entire ordeal that will unfold.

Albert attempted to tackle a problem of gigantic magnitude. His job included visiting care facilities and assessing and engineering solutions to fix what wasn't working from places that had 40 percent prevalence of HIV to very, very rich provinces across South Africa. Albert learned about the broad spectrum of issues and it is not a simple issue. Nothing ever is. Albert finally realized he was not moving the needle.

"It's probably the most difficult decision I've ever had to make—to leave. I still feel like it's a personal failure."

Albert got emotional thinking back to that early morning in KwaZulu Natal before sunrise. The area had the highest prevalence of HIV in the country. Although the healthcare facility opened at seven thirty a.m., the line usually started as early as five thirty a.m. It was pitch dark, but all these patients were already in line, waiting to get treated. The area was very religious. As the staff was preparing to open the facility, they started singing a hymn together.

At that point, Albert had already decided to leave and was overwhelmed by guilt; that was when he saw a pair of green eyes almost glowing in the dark, looking toward him.

"I thought he was looking straight at me, and I was looking into his eyes; but then I realized he wasn't really seeing me. He was blind." The man had severe retinopathy, maybe from HIV or diabetes. Under the moonless, starless sky, the sound of the hymn echoed around the facility. What does it take to bring light to a situation like this? Those green eyes pierced through Albert's heart that was leaking with utter powerlessness.

Spoiler alert: if you choose to go down the path that is the second phase of life, sooner or later you will hit a rock bottom of biblical proportion. It's part of the process that leads to personal growth and actualization, and the pain is inevitable. Snoozing after you receive your wake-up call gives you the time and space to prepare yourself for the big adventure. It's okay to snooze.

We will come back to Albert's story. But first, let's learn how to recognize another type of wake-up call.

## A MORE SUBTLE SIGN

Just because your sign did not come as a big bang doesn't mean the package was not delivered. But, of course, it's always your choice whether to sign for the package or reject it.

For most of us, the sign is subtle. It's like living in a *slightly* haunted house. Every now and then, you hear a suspicious sound, see a shadow, or find some weird coincidences. You never walk into the kitchen and witness the drawers being pulled out and utensils flying in the air. You can't be sure there's a ghost, and it's not enough to convince you to make a move immediately, but you definitely feel like you're losing your mind day by day.

If you're thinking, "Um, I don't believe in ghosts," fine.

Then look within and ask yourself this: are you living a separate, compartmentalized life like you're a double agent or have a split personality?

Most of us are likely to fulfil the TM (Talent-Market) combo in our jobs because if you're not skillful and talented in your job, you'd get fired, and if you're not getting paid, you'd probably fire your boss. Many of us compromise by fulfilling the PM (Passion-Mission) combo outside of our day jobs.

In fact, many of us end up compartmentalizing our waking hours in four ways. The TM (Talent-Market) combo is typically that default first job/career choice; TP (Talent-Passion) is what we do as our hobby; PM (Passion-Mission) is where we do our volunteering and charity work; and the MM (Mission-Market) combo is likely a pet project you have on the side. For example, one of my best friends is a litigator by day and became involved with a group of friends to create a face mask manufacturing company at the beginning of the COVID-19 pandemic. They saw an urgent need and gap in the market for kid-sized protective face masks.

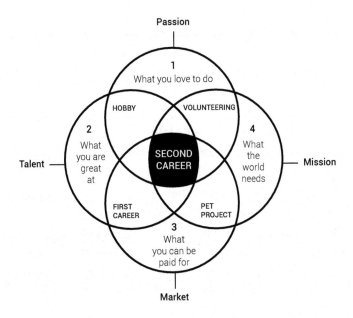

People used to always ask me why and how I did so many different things outside of work when I already had very long hours and a high-stress job. I used to think I was just ridiculously curious and wanted to explore as many things as possible at the same time. It turned out it's because I couldn't fulfill anything other than the TM combo at work, so I had to do the other combos elsewhere.

That restlessness inspired me and my friends to start a group called Afterwork Power. The group aimed to empower career professionals to find and express their passions and meaning after working hours, quite literally. But over time, I couldn't find contentment. I wanted to build a life more coherent and spend those many working hours every day doing things that aligned with my values.

Having said that, I did spend more than a decade living a split life. I can't talk about the split personality syndrome without introducing you to Karuna Warren.

## HAVING A FOOT IN BOTH CAMPS

Bali, 2016: after almost everyone I'd met in Ubud told me I must try Ecstatic Dance, I finally decided to check it out at the infamous Yoga Barn. When I arrived before the scheduled class time, I found a long queue already formed below the elevated hut where the class was to be held, and I was told the hut was already at full capacity and they were not allowing more people in. Disappointed and irritated by the hot weather as well as what seemed to be a wasted trip, I went to the café area for a cold juice.

That's where I met Karuna. Or I should say, that's where I was *meant* to meet Karuna.

Sitting across the table from me was a tribal, ten-years-younger version of Denzel Washington.

We could not have looked more dissimilar. Karuna was tall with dark skin and very deep, sad eyes. He exuded raw, somewhat mysterious energy. Karuna stood out from the crowd, even in Ubud, with heavy accessories on his face and hands and Native American-patterned clothing. I was this short, Chinese, metropolitan girl wearing a designer Mala that obviously didn't come from a guru but came with a six-month warranty and was paid for with my credit card.

But we somehow started talking. Surprisingly, Karuna and I are "same-same," a phrase I had learned from the Balinese.

Just like me, Karuna was taking a career break. At that point, he had been living in two worlds for eight years, something I could resonate with, as I'd also been moving one foot into a different world while keeping the other firmly in the corporate safe haven for about seven years since my first diagnosis of chronic depression. Karuna's two worlds were more drastically different.

Karuna was an engineer specializing in environmental engineering with twenty years of experience. He has Native American blood in him from his father's side, but his family was never really spiritual in his childhood. It was not until 2005 when Karuna first experienced a ceremony at the Native American church that he was fundamentally moved and started exploring a spiritual path.

Corporate America, as Karuna puts it, provided him with a stable fat paycheck, and his work was also somehow related to his passion: the environment. After spending years in the industry and developing an expertise, Karuna did not find joy in his very successful career. The higher he climbed, the clearer the view was: the hard cold truth that the system is too strong and the utilities superpowers and vested interests are too strong. As an environmental engineer, Karuna's hands were tied in terms of how much good or impact he could really bring while still working within the system.

In the meantime, Karuna would go off every weekend to participate in his church's Native American ceremonies, where he gradually took official roles such as the fire keeper. These ceremonies commonly last all night, often starting Saturday night and ending Sunday morning. Karuna would spend these weekends singing, drumming, dancing, scripture reading, praying, and sharing ideas with his spiritual family. Chewing peyote buttons and drinking peyote tea are central practices of the Native American church as well. Outsiders commonly think of peyote as simply a means of getting high, but those who use it for religious purposes see it as sacramental. The cactus is understood to be sacred, and ingestion of the plant brings the user into a closer understanding of the spiritual world (Beyer, 2020).

Going off to these ceremonies every weekend and coming back to his office in Corporate America, Karuna was torn between the two different worlds. The contradiction between the energy in the office of enclosed concrete with central air conditioning and the grounded-ness and connectedness with the earth and nature in open air mixed with the smell of campfire and peyote was becoming more and more unsettling. After eight years of living this double life (can you believe how long it took?), Karuna took a career break to travel.

## NOT ALL WHO WANDER ARE LOST

When I met Karuna in Bali, he was on a twenty-one-day journey to water spaces in nature to meditate and listen.

He told me about his serendipitous encounter with a Buddhist sage.

Karuna found this sage meditating downstream from a waterfall. Coming out of his meditation, the sage opened his eyes and looked at Karuna with a huge smile on his face. Karuna started smiling too and asked for the sage's name. The sage began laughing but didn't answer. Karuna, too, started laughing. The two men just sat there and laughed with their hearts, bellies, and full bodies engaged until a hummingbird came near them and seemed to be suspended in time.

The two strangers naturally started to meditate together. After an hour of sitting and breathing together under the waterfall, Karuna asked, "Why did you laugh when I asked for your name?"

"I don't identify with titles after liberation—not even names— so I couldn't remember," the sage replied.

"I'm Karuna. Nice to meet you," said Karuna.

"I'm Karuna also. Nice meeting you. We are same-same," the sage said.

They both started laughing again until Karuna found himself crying.

Feeling the deep wisdom from this laughing sage, Karuna asked him, "Am I going the right direction by leaving my original world?"

The sage smiled, "No wrong way, just right now."

That day, Karuna left with this advice from the sage, "Connect with your heart and inner child. He knows getting lost is okay too."

You may also have woken up to the call of your soul and become interested in balancing a pure secular life with a spiritual pursuit. But there's no on-off switch; there's no quick crossover. Look at Albert, look at Karuna, and look at me. Don't feel bad for taking what seems to be a never-ending amount of time to switch lanes.

Most people stay on the path they are already on, even if it is going nowhere. It's actually a good sign if you found yourself snoozing and starting to wander without knowing exactly where that wandering would lead you after receiving your first wake-up call. You are wandering, but not lost.

It takes years to gradually shed the past, those extra layers, and let go of all sorts of attachments before one can be ready to make that big bang change. Especially if one used to have a "successful" life; becoming unattached and taking the leap to pursue something bigger takes time.

You are receiving and contemplating.

## THE FUCK-IT MOMENT

Here's a sneak peek into what the big bang looks like when it actually happens.

To be honest, it's a bit of an anticlimax.

Once again, my utterly unscientific research methodology has led me to this conclusion: there are three types of fuck-it moments.

One: having kids. And interestingly, usually it takes the *second* kid to do the trick. "We had our second kid, and I said, if I don't make a change now, I'm never going to make the change." This was Albert. I suspect that by the *second* kid, you are really cementing yourself into a certain way of life unless you deliberately try to break away from that societal expectation.

I've heard a similar fuck-it moment from Francis Ngai, the "father of social enterprise" in Hong Kong.

Francis "followed the script" of do well in school, get a good job, and then climb the ladder. With a background in advertisement and marketing, Francis's last corporate job was at PCCW, a telecommunication giant with businesses all over the world from broadband internet to mobile network to media. Francis was the head of strategy in developing PCCW's China IT businesses. That script to success had an unexpected twist in the form of a "dough." Francis recalled holding his newborn for the first time, tears running down his cheeks and his entire system shocked by experiencing the creation of life:

"This dough can be molded into anything. Do I want my children to have dreams? Yes, I do. But then I had to take a hard, honest look at myself and ask, 'Do *I* have dreams?' No, I didn't. I was only making rich people richer. That's when I realized I needed to be a better role model for my children."

In 2005, Francis had a daughter; in 2006, he had a son; and in 2007, he quit his scripted path of twelve years and embarked on a brand-new adventure of social entrepreneurship. Francis has been a father figure to me on this less travelled path. He has become a role model for many, not only his two kids.

The second type of fuck-it moment is a bit less obvious: the *threat* of becoming even more successful in the conventional sense. That's what I had. I was *threatened* with a potential promotion. I knew if I took one more step up the corporate ladder, that would be it. I would never have the guts to give it all up and pursue something more meaningful.

Isabelle Decitre, now CEO of venture capital company ID Capital with a focus on sustainable and disruptive food solutions in Asia-Pacific, told me something very similar. "It was as if I had a red carpet rolled out for me," she recalled. After twenty years in the luxury goods world—having held executive positions at LVMH, Hennessy, and Cartier, just to name a few—Isabelle was thinking of her next move. A few dream job offers were just waiting for her to say yes. Nobody in their right mind could have turned down those offers, but none of them were matching her dream of a different kind of adventure in Asia. That's when she feared it was now or never. She was a mother of three young kids, by the way. But in 2012, ditching the red carpet, Isabelle moved from Paris to

Singapore for nothing other than guaranteed uncertainties. By the end of 2016, ID Capital had launched Future Food Asia, a first-of-its-kind venture investment and open innovation platform for the food and agriculture technology sector.

Finally, the third kind is a debilitating incident. And that was the fuck-it moment Karuna had.

Having run out of money by the end of his traveling, Karuna thought he had done his freedom trip and should go back to Corporate America. He got a job and worked at integrating himself back into the system. After about four months with the heightened self-awareness from his soul-searching trip, he knew he was stuck in the wrong job. But what was truly amazing was the stuck-ness manifested in him physically.

With zero ambiguity, the universe sent Karuna a message. While still struggling with the quit-not-quit dilemma, Karuna woke up one day with half of his face paralyzed.

He was told it was Bell's palsy. What caused it? Unknown. How to cure it? It is a relatively rare condition that only happens to twenty-three out one hundred thousand people. It is a neurological disorder where one of the facial nerves is damaged. Medicine only helps soothe some of the symptoms, and it can take weeks to see the first movements in the face resumed. Full recovery never happens for about 30 percent of cases (Marson and Salinas, 2000). Told to not panic but also not to expect immediate improvements and reassured there was no way to switch back the facial nerve at once, Karuna relied on his faith to carry him through.

Using a holistic approach and tapping into his inner source of healing, Karuna went through plant medicines and acupuncture, prayers and sweat lodges. With help from his "spirit helpers and angels and earthly friends," on day thirty, Karuna could close his eye fully and his full smile was returning.

"Sometimes one has to hurl oneself into the abyss with surrender only to discover it's a feather bed," said Karuna. With much gratitude for his newfound health and the spiritual lessons learned, he finally Q-U-I-T.

Karuna embarked on a journey to move to Costa Rica to build an eco-village of his dreams: a conscious community that takes care of the environment and each other.

"Some won't understand, and I don't have a ton of money, but it's okay," said Karuna.

"Same-same," I said.

It's been a blessing for me to have met Karuna and witnessed his journey. I suspect we met because I needed to follow his story for the years that have since passed and for more years to come to keep me encouraged and on track to fall into this deeper way of living. I also suspect we met so I can share Karuna's story with you.

We may receive different signs; it may take each of us different steps and time frames to dissolve our first phase way of life, and we may have very different fuck-it moments. If we choose to get on the path of evolution, we're all more "same-same" than we think. You are not alone in this.

## CHAPTER 3

# THE COURAGE TO QUIT

———

*"Our deepest fear is not that we are inadequate.
Our deepest fear is that we are powerful beyond
measure. It is our light, not our darkness that most
frightens us...And as we let our own light shine,
we unconsciously give other people permission to
do the same. As we are liberated from our own
fear, our presence automatically liberates others."*

—MARIANNE WILLIAMSON

Are you afraid of heights? I am.

"Get me out of here!" I cried. I was literally bawling my eyes
out and stomping the ground like a child pulling a tantrum.

My nine-to-thrive workshop coach, Lydia Lee, had brought
me to a treetop adventure park for a "fun outing." Yes, there
was a workshop tailored for corporate professionals wanting
to quit their nine-to-five and turn a new page in their careers.

It was a fine day and we were surrounded by a greenwood of trees in one of Bali's largest botanical gardens. Other than our class of potential corporate quitters, there were many families and groups of friends just having a fun day of adventure. I saw kids flying around the trees like monkeys. As I was crying out of fear, there were six-year-olds looking at me and laughing at me like I was crazy.

"You think you're so brave?" I wanted to say to those mean kids. "Your lack of fear now is just because you've got nothing to lose. Wait and see—thirty years from now, when you are my age, see if you become an even bigger wuss than I am."

Suspended bridges, spider nets, Tarzan jumps, flying swings, a total of sixty-five "fun challenges": did I die and go to hell? I was supposed to hoist, jump, and balance from one tree to another using a harness to clip myself onto the wires between the trees. There were six different circuits from the smallest to biggest (highest) challenge, starting with a Yellow Squirrel circuit for four- to six-year-olds right up to the thrilling Black Adrenalin circuit.

"I hate you, Lydia!" I yelled. Lydia didn't care; she had enough experience with fear-bound corporate professionals who said they wanted to change but were paralyzed by fear. There's a reason Lydia put us through that hell. It's not enough to talk about fear in a classroom setting. "Learning a concept intellectually is very different from getting it at a body, mind, and spirit level; this trail gives you a molecular-level understanding of fear and how to work with that fear," said Lydia.

The idea was to keep progressing even when it's scary. Fear dissipates through progressive action of gradually levelling up from Yellow Squirrel to Black Adrenalin.

All of my suppressed fear burst out of my body in tears and screams at that hell park.

Looking at those levels of circuits from two to twenty meters from the ground, I suddenly got it. Why does it take so long— as in so many years—for career professionals to go from the wake-up call to the fuck-it moment? Why did it take me seven long years to finally call it quits? Why was I so consumed by paralyzing fear?

Because it's like starting at the Black Adrenalin level right away.

We've climbed so high in our first career. The opportunity cost is as high as twenty meters from the ground, if not more. If we change gears then, there seems to be no way to go but down. It will be a steep fall because we have way too much to lose.

## QUITTING WHILE YOU ARE AT THE TOP OF YOUR GAME

You may have a reputation to maintain. Luckily, I was enough of a nobody that I didn't have that concern, but the income level and social status that came with my profession were enough to deter me from destroying that foundation of a socially applauded upper-middle-class bright future I was heading toward.

Some people think quitting is easy. Quitting while failing may be easy. Quitting while winning is anything but.

For a public display of quitting while winning, look no further than the Netflix documentary on ARASHI.

ARASHI, a Japanese five-member male idol group whose name means "storm," debuted in 1999 as teenagers.

Fast forward to 2019: in the midst of their twenty-year anniversary tour with a total of fifty performances and an anticipated 2,375,000 concertgoers, making it the largest anniversary tour in Japanese music history, ARASHI announced the band would go on hiatus effective end of 2020.

Right before announcing their planned hiatus, ARASHI reached epic levels of fame and fortune that most artists only dream of. It officially became the best-selling boy band in Asia, with sold-out tours to over fourteen million fans and over fifty-four million albums sold (Stock, 2020). Its success spread beyond music and spanned various genres, including hosting its own prime time variety shows on television and each member shining in other arenas from news broadcasting to acting in Oscar award-winning films (Fuji Television Network, 2021; IMDb, 2021).

Nowadays, with K-pop culture gaining a global following— for example, Korean male idol group BTS made history by winning Top Sales Artist and Top Sales Song at the Billboard Music Awards in 2021—this "business model" has become more familiar to the public in the West (McIntyre, 2021). Make no mistake, it is brutal. In both J-pop and K-pop, there has been a decades-old, well-established training system to churn out pop idols.

Trainees, as they are called, are typically accepted into intensive training programs as early as the age of twelve. They receive training in the form of vocal lessons to different styles of dancing to different language courses (to expand beyond the domestic market). Many try to juggle school at the same time for as long as they can. They might have one day off every fortnight from the training program. These kids live a childhood—if you can still call it that—like the title of one of BTS's hit songs, "Blood Sweat & Tears" (HYBE LABELS, 2016). Most are eliminated over the years, leaving the top of the top to debut either as solo artists or in different group formations.

The hard work doesn't stop after the debut. In a period of twenty years, ARASHI has created twenty-two albums and has fifty-four number-one hits to its name (Oricon, 2020). Just to put things in perspective, Adele debuted in 2008. In a period of thirteen years, she has released a total of three albums (Official Charts, 2021).

Satoshi Ohno is the oldest member (and therefore the leader of the group, according to tradition) in ARASHI. At the age of thirty-eight, he revealed he was the one who initiated the discussion with his band mates about his desire to leave the entertainment industry.

"I want to live freely," Ohno said, "to see views that I've never seen" (Kyodo News, 2019).

## HOW WE CAME TO ACHIEVE SUCCESS WE LATER RE-SENT

Ohno used to love being cooped up inside and drawing. But in 1994, he joined Johnny & Associates talent agency and started being trained in singing and dancing. Ohno was a high school dropout then; Johnny Kitagawa was like the godfather of Japan's music industry. Between drawing at home and becoming a singer managed by Johnny's agency, it was clear what had more prospects.

This is exactly how we often come to achieve success we later resent.

After working full-time at Johnny's theatre production organization for two years since the age of sixteen, Ohno wanted to quit. "I totally burned out from it," Ohno said in the Netflix documentary.

Ohno wanted to become an illustrator, so for three years, he drew and drew. "Even if it doesn't turn into a real job, I want to keep drawing," Ohno told Johnny. Johnny never said yes or no to Ohno's resignation.

For a few years, the ambiguity continued. Ohno would be "helping out" at Johnny's agency, dancing, sometimes singing parts of a song, until one day, Ohno suddenly found himself assigned to a boy band with a set date to debut.

When he told his mother, she cried her eyes out from joy and relief.

"She cried really hard," Ohno remembered. "I had nothing. When I saw my mom cry, I realized I got a job."

"It's been twenty years since that," said Ohno.

Most of us are good at, or at least can pull off, more than one thing. Whether it's a teacher or mentor or someone experienced in a certain trade or profession, someone would see what they recognize as talent within us. When coupled with opportunity on offer—like when the godfather of the Japanese music industry insists you join the new boy band he's launching—naturally, there's almost no reason to say no. That may turn out to be your life or twenty years of your life—your first career.

That's what any responsible career guidance counselor would advise you. When my counselor looked at me at the age of seventeen, a mostly-A student who represented the school on the debate team, asking if I should go to law school or study fine art (I did fine in art class, sure), what on earth was she supposed to say?

"It's fine to have dreams, but you have to be realistic," my guidance counselor advised.

So we end up starting a smaller, safer version of what our careers, or indeed our lives, could be.

That is how we then develop the existential crisis that is "typical of modern societies in which people do what they are told to do, or what others do, rather than what they want to do," as Héctor García and Francesc Miralles describe in *Ikigai: The*

*Japanese Secret to a Long and Happy Life.* "They then often try to fill the gap between what is expected of them and what they want for themselves with economic power or physical pleasure, or by numbing their senses."

## BECOMING THE CAPRICIOUS QUITTER

There is nothing wrong with following the norm and taking the safer route in that first phase of life, but are those wins under your belt bracing you for the bigger, much deeper second phase of life? Or are they pinning you down to settle for less?

I wonder how Ohno's mom reacted to him quitting ARASHI.

She cried her eyes out when he joined, overjoyed that he had found his footing in this world. Twenty years later, he's been so publicly successful. Was that enough? Or did she cry again, this time out of anguish?

Because my mom certainly cried out of anguish.

With me playing my depression card, my mom has tried her best to be supportive of my "reckless" life choices. I can imagine how she felt when I quit my lawyering career. Disappointment doesn't even begin to describe it.

Quitting something everyone thinks you *should* want, that everyone thinks you *should* be content with, grateful for, and happy about, apparently makes you selfish, rash, and capricious.

In ARASHI's press conference in 2019 announcing their hiatus, a reporter asked whether the band's decision to cease activities was "irresponsible."

Imagination goes wild in my head about what my mom thought of me. I was swallowed in guilt and shame underneath, but on the surface, I got triggered easily and reacted to the slightest hint of despise in her words or her facial expressions. I was often angry; I was also very afraid. Unfortunately, my whole life I've been seeking others' approval, especially my mother's. For the first few years, I didn't say my choice was definite. I always just referred to it as me taking a break to try other things—much like ARASHI calling its break a "hiatus." Everyone pretty much knows it meant the end, not a pause.

I remember one day walking in on my mom sobbing at our dining table.

"What have I done wrong?" she asked.

"We spent so much money on your education. Did we not support you in every single way we could? You graduated from a top university, worked at the top law firms. What the hell happened?"

I had no words.

I would have fought back if it had been the usual, "Your cousin must be earning three, four times what you earn now," or "They're getting their third investment property," or "My friend's son is getting married. Both of them are bankers."

But this time, I could see my mom was hurting deeply. It went beyond just jealousy and bitterness. Her heart was broken for what *her* life had turned out to be. Even though she had her own career, one people would call successful, her daughter was supposed to be a big part of her life accomplishments too. I did not live up to her expectation—far from it.

"You're working your ass off and earning less than what you earned fresh out of college. Do you know how much your cousin is earning now? He only graduated a few years ago. But he chose something sensible, didn't he? Whereas my daughter decided to be a dreamer. What you are earning is *despicable*. It's a despicable income." Mom could hardly enunciate, trying to catch her breaths between the sobbing.

"How did I end up raising a loser?" she asked, hitting her chest in an attempt to turn that emotional agony into something she could feel and hopefully physically dissolve.

## THE BURDENS WE INHERIT

My mum was the eldest of five kids. She was always studying while her siblings ran around being kids. My mum graduated top of her high school. Back in the days when only a handful of students from each high school ever got into university, she did. Despite her passion for literature, she picked a "practical" degree in social science. She spent her whole career of over three decades in the government—a notoriously stable and high-paying working environment. Before she had her own family, her paychecks went to supporting her parents and siblings. After having me and my sister, her paychecks went to supporting us.

Dream? What dream?

My mum, Ohno's mum, same-same. They diligently fulfilled their missions in life as daughters and mothers. They had dreams too, but they sacrificed them to give their children the best and as much as possible prepare them for success.

And now I'm saying success is not good enough for me? What is my mum supposed to feel about it?

Mengzi, also known as Mencius (372–289 BC), was a Chinese Confucian philosopher who has been described as the "Second Sage" after only Confucius himself. His mother is often held up as an exemplary mother figure in Chinese culture. Ask any Chinese person, they would have heard of her stories; few would know her name. She's literally just known as Mother Meng. She is the golden standard of how one should bring up their offspring. Her most famous story is one of moving houses three times before finding a location she felt was a proper environment for her child to dedicate himself to being educated. Side note: she was a widow living in poverty; it's not like she had nothing better to do but be a helicopter mom. That story is so embedded in Chinese culture that it is an idiom (Chan, 1963).

Yes, a lot is expected from parents in Chinese culture, and that is true for many Asian cultures and beyond. Similarly, a lot is also expected from the children. Why are Asian kids getting full marks in SATs, acing math tests wherever they are in the world, and always winning those national school science contests? We are not prodigies. Asian children are simply expected to study hard and get good grades. It's always been that way—since Mengzi's time and long before that. "It's fine to have dreams, but you have to be realistic," we are often told.

Another lesson from Mother Meng is that quitting is damned. Once Mengzi was living in an environment deemed suitable for him to flourish by his mom, Mengzi started receiving a formal education. One day, Mengzi skipped school to play. After Mengzi returned home, he saw Mother Meng, filled with sadness and anger. She picked up a pair of scissors and started cutting the piece of brocade she had worked so hard on for days. As the cloth cut in half fell on the ground, Mengzi knelt to the ground and asked his mom why.

Mother Meng replied, "Weaving is working inch by inch, building it up to a foot, and finally into a whole roll of cloth. A piece of cloth cut in the middle is useless. If you don't study hard now, you'll grow up to be like the brocade I just cut: useless."

Now that is a classic story to illustrate the importance of being diligent, persisting, and seeing things through no matter what. Quitting halfway? You useless piece of shit. So much fun growing up that way, right?

I've spoken with enough people to learn that quitting is easier for some and much more difficult for others. The pattern I observe comes down to a person's upbringing. Some cultures are what I'd call very "unforgiving." Generally, these are the cultures where the parents never ever let go of their children and have serious boundary issues. I'm brought up in the

Chinese culture and can attest to that, and from my research and interviews, Japanese, Korean, and Indian: same-same.

Hasan Minhaj, a comedian and *Daily Show* correspondent, was born in America with parents from India. In the beginning of trying to build up his career as a comedian, he was given an ultimatum from his dad to follow his sister's lead and go to law school. "As an immigrant child, that's what's expected of you," Hasan recalled. "It's the dream of every immigrant parent for their child to become a doctor, a lawyer, or an engineer." His parents were concerned he was going to struggle to provide for his family. Note that at that point, he did not actually have his own family yet. In many Asian cultures, "family" is a wide concept. It covers upward generation(s), downward generation(s), and possibly sideways too. "Whatever it is, invest in yourself. You'll reap exponential rewards from that later," said Hasan's father (Vee, 2017).

There is quite a clear distinction among people I've interviewed. Those who didn't go through a huge struggle in quitting and following a less travelled path grew up in households where they were encouraged to "follow their dreams" and told "they can be whatever they want to be." Those from more "unforgiving" upbringings, which can go beyond culture into the family's social status and lineage, tend to have a lot of ingrained guilt and shame around failing to carry the family name or even the pride of their race on their shoulders.

## UNSUBSCRIBING FROM SUCCESSISM

Two months after the hiatus announcement, ARASHI was still going full speed, fulfilling its promise to fans that it would give its all and end with a big bang.

But the end was expected. Ohno prepared for his solo art exhibition. He was painting a face. It was taller than him and almost as big as half of a wall in his studio. He was listening to ARASHI music while painting the face of Johnny who had died at the age of eighty-seven a few months after ARASHI's announcement.

"To be honest, I didn't cry when Johnny died," said Ohno.

Did Johnny, the father of Japan's music industry, agree with Ohno's decision to quit? Or did he try to stop Ohno like he did twenty years ago?

Thinking back to how he basically passively fell into a career that lasted for twenty years, Ohno said, "I could not just quit. I have responsibility to the group." Then he wept and asked, as if Johnny could still hear him, "Why the heck did you die?"

There was a deep sadness in Ohno's eyes. For a star as big as he is and the leader of one of the most successful boy bands in history, Ohno has a timidness and vulnerability to him that's hard to explain.

Maybe we can see into his weeping inner child through his paintings. Maybe we can even see why his inner child is weeping. Sitting on a small stool, Ohno worked on his canvas on the floor. The painting was big, but his strokes were small. Stroke by stroke, he seemed to be lost in another world, painting each stroke with so much care and tenderness. I don't know the first thing about appreciating an illustrative art, but there's something very moving watching Ohno paint. It's simply an authentic expression of who he is. He may never reach the same level of success as an illustrator compared to his identity of being part of ARASHI, but this is just a part of his truth he has been putting on hold or hiding for twenty years. This is just something he has to do—not for the sake of being successful.

But sadness is often not enough when you are carrying so many people's expectations, hopes, and dreams on your shoulders.

A lot of us were raised with an obligation to succeed.

It's our basic duty.

Not just for ourselves—in fact, mostly for others, it seems. We are not to let down our parents, our family, our colleagues, our mentors, our country, our race, and our gender. God forbid if we decide not to conform to that societal narrative of successism. That imprint is so powerful; many a time, it feels not just cultural but ancestral. To this day, years into my journey into my second phase vocation, I'm still fighting that shadow.

What is the courage to quit?

It is knowing your own truth enough to unsubscribe from the norm and the default if it's not true for you. It is recognizing the success that leaves you feeling empty inside is not what you want to settle for. It is reconciling with the shame and guilt that comes with disappointing those closest to you, risking losing their approval and love, and forging the path your soul is calling for. It is transforming generations upon generations of expectations and conditioning into bigger hopes and dreams.

Cultivating that courage to quit is the first step into the second phase of life.

Brace yourself. The journey begins.

# PART II

# EVOLUTION

## CHAPTER 4

# IN PURSUIT OF HIPPINESS

———

*"The purpose of life is not to be happy. It
is to be useful, to be honorable, to be
compassionate, to have it make some difference
that you have lived and lived well."*

–RALPH WALDO EMERSON

The second phase of life begins. It's a frigging jungle. You will walk through the jungle of trees with gigantic boughs reaching up to the sky like haunted limbs, looming over and projecting shadows of all shapes and forms. The shadows devouring everything they touch. The deeper into the jungle, the darker it gets, and who knows what else is lurking in the uncanny darkness.

Some damn rain of biblical proportions will come down on you for as long as it takes. You will be exhausted. Everything you thought essential that you carried with you has to be let go. You will not be able to move forward and find your way out of this maze of turmoil unless you keep unloading the baggage. Even your clothes become soaked and so heavy that they begin to drag and sink you into the ground. You have no choice but to let go of that final layer shielding and masking you from the world.

The jungle is metaphorical, but everything you will encounter in the second phase of life is very much like what I just described.

You will confront shadows—only they are your own.

You will have to let go of a lot of baggage: physical stuff, emotional issues, habitual patterns, and beliefs.

At this stage, if you choose to cross the threshold with the courage to quit, you are leaving your "original world." So here we are, at the second act of your life journey, where everything starts to become even more messy.

After tossing the life script handed down to you, you will go through a life detoxification process. To continue this journey, you will have to consciously and consistently unsubscribe from societal expectations and norms to create your own story untainted by old conditionings and imprints.

Watch me do it by trying to turn into a hippie.

## OPEN HEART SURGERY

Wait, how does being a hippie have anything to do with my second phase of life?

I didn't plan it. But in hindsight, it all made sense.

It all started with me finding my yoga teacher.

This was not a "yoga teacher" in the sense that I went to a hot yoga class every Thursday at my local gym or yoga center where I had a monthly membership or class coupons. No disrespect to all the yoga teachers who taught me before; you opened my eyes to the amazing life philosophy that is yoga. But when holding down a corporate job, I could only do group classes, weekend yoga festivals, and maybe weeklong yoga retreats once or twice a year. It was very different from being able to live and breathe yoga every day, being a full-time student, and working at it like a full-time job. Being able to leave "home" and immerse myself into an environment conducive to studying yoga was one of the greatest blessings of my life.

After quitting my job, I totally thought I'd join an ashram and live there for a few months, but life had a different plan for me. My teacher turned out to be a traveling yogi.

Throughout my first career in that tiny work and social bubble where everybody looked mass-produced from the same cookie cutter, most people were connected by one common life goal: retirement. That was the light at the end of the tunnel driving us forward every day. We would talk about our dreams of opening a café by the sea one day: after we retired, writing a book; after we retired, traveling the world; after we retired, being happy—after we retired.

It was beyond refreshing to meet someone who had no aspiration to retire whatsoever. He was sixty-eight years old when we met. I thought, *this guy must be doing something right with his life if he loves his work so much.*

Peter, who turned out to be the yoga teacher life gifted me, had been practicing, teaching, and living yoga for more than fifty years. He's not going to like me telling you this, but he looked like Yoda. Let me add this: a *younger* Yoda. He was not green, but he had the same eyes and gaze—purity and innocence mixed with a deep contentment. Now imagine Yoda owning and running a restaurant and investing in real estate through flipping properties. These were just some of the lines of work Peter had been engaged in through his adult life when he had a family to support.

Most of his younger adult life was spent in India in the sixties, learning from and living with some of the greatest gurus. Having studied with different yoga lineages over the decades, in the later part of his life, he chose *Anahata Yoga* to pass on to the next generation of teachers and students. He was the only one left from his guru's handful of disciples still alive and teaching.

There are certain encounters in life that just feel like destiny. For me, meeting Peter was one of those encounters. *Anahata* is the heart chakra in the yogic tradition. It is the fourth chakra of the spiritual body associated with goodness, kindness, compassion, empathy, altruism, and unconditional love.

Peter was trained in this form of yoga in the Himalaya mountains; his guru lived in a temple near the border between India and China. The sequence was quite different from anything I had ever seen. There seemed to be an influence from Tai Chi or Qigong. The yoga form flowed very deeply with the breath. Sometimes it was a graceful dance with energy; sometimes it felt like a powerful play with *qi* (the word for life force in Chinese medicine and philosophy).

Unlike many of the more well-known *asanas* (the word for body posture in yoga) like a downward-facing dog or a tree pose where you go into, hold, and move out of the posture, the practice with Peter was more like a dance. The *asana* was more of a constant movement that sometimes felt like there was really no beginning or end to one pose. The whole journey was the pose. It was a connected, looped circle of dance. Some of these unusual movements could be difficult to grasp at first, and it's hard to create very precise descriptive instructions. But the weirdest thing was I felt that my body already knew some of the movements, like there was muscle memory from another lifetime or some other parallel dimension. There were arm movements I had been doing since I was a kid, like stretches I often naturally expressed without having to learn them. I was then discovering my natural moves in this form of yoga sequence.

Discovering *Anahata Yoga* was like finding home at a deep subconscious level, and it taught me that feeling in the gut when you find something that's meant to be—something that's your calling, your mission, your purpose in life. That "coming home" feeling would continue to guide me in trusting my own GPS, that inner guidance and truth.

During the standard two-hundred-hour yoga teacher training led by Peter, I was living and spending most of the day with our group of fewer than twenty people for more than a month in a beautiful, secluded town called Hallein in Austria. We practiced Sun Salutation in the garden under an apple tree, we practiced *pranayama* on the mountain, and we meditated at the lake. Nature helped to wash away some of my imprints and baggage from life. At the same time, I saw Peter healing the hurt in others in the class through yoga philosophy, sharing his life experiences, and guiding us to see our own light and shadow.

Halfway through the training, Peter asked me, "Your heart chakra is completely stuck. Why are you not opening your heart?"

"I'm heartbroken," I said.

"Your heart is not broken; no one can break your heart unless you choose to believe that your heart is in pieces. Feel your heartbeat. Feel your heart in your chest. It's there. It's in one piece, is it not?" said Peter. I sobbed and sobbed while Peter sat there and simply held the space for me with a lot of compassion.

Epiphanies are often not experienced with the mind. Verbal discussions and analysis would have only dumbed down a level of understanding that could not be comprehended through thoughts. As we sat facing the same direction and meditated, I was transported to a different realm. Peter held out his hands, and without actual contact, I felt a strong stream of *qi* flowing through my back. I could feel the energy filling me up. It was powerful and overwhelming but not intimidating. It was more accurate to describe that I *saw* the light instead of I *felt* it, and it gradually became all of me until it quite literally broke my heart open. I *saw* the light break through my heart area and turn into a sunflower opening from my chest.

I was shocked at whatever it was that had just happened.

"It's not me," said Peter. "You are the only person who can decide that you will open your heart again." And that was that.

## LETTING GO 1.0

After I resigned from my corporate job in 2014, in the beginning, headhunters kept calling me for interviews to get me back into the same bubble of finance and law. I wanted to break out of that circle. What's out there? In a metropolis like Hong Kong, there were not many role models I could think of except for David Yeung, who founded Green Monday, a social enterprise that promotes a plant-based diet.

Three weeks after I quit, I was sitting in a street corner café in my neighborhood with a few friends just hanging, not knowing what the universe had in store for me that day. Then, boom! A guy walked by the café. He looked familiar. Oh my god! My mind went blank, my jaw dropped, and my eyes went wide looking out the window toward this person. Seeing me completely losing it, my friends turned in the same direction, and one of them decided to start waving. In hindsight, I owe her a big thank-you.

Now the guy was looking toward us and wondering who these people were. I had to decide what to do. Utterly embarrassed, I ran out of the café and went up to this guy. And of course, I decided to further embarrass myself with, "Hi...are you...David? You don't know me, but...I've admired you for a long time..."

Classic stalker introduction.

It was David Yeung, the icon of the plant-based movement in Hong Kong, the person I'd been trying to connect with through the nine degrees of separation. I'm not sure whether David was overly curious or utterly reckless, but he actually decided to chat with me and exchanged contacts instead of calling the police. There we were, degrees of separation gone. My amazing stalker-style elevator pitch should have guaranteed the story ended there, but a few days later, I got a call from David to meet at his office. I was offered a job and the rest is history. Actually, not quite. That was the beginning of the rest of my life and the stories you are now reading here.

I went to the yoga teacher training in Austria I had planned before I quite literally ran into my next job on the street. I came back from Austria to Hong Kong to work at this social startup as employee number twelve.

But soon I was in a dilemma.

Although I had gathered the courage to quit my job and even landed on a new job amazingly quickly, I was so depleted of energy and enthusiasm that it felt impossible to forge a new path.

Although I had gathered the courage to quit, the internal work was not yet done. The shame and the guilt would have continued to drown me if I didn't work through my internal conflicts and struggles. To move forward, I had to sever that deeply embedded link of self-worth with societal approval.

Full disclosure: there's also this other thing.

Peter, my yoga teacher, and I fell in love.

As destiny would have it, that moment happened on the exact same street that I ran into David.

A few months after I started working for David, I found myself standing outside that same street corner café in my neighborhood again just hanging—this time with Peter—not knowing what the universe had in store for me that day.

Peter flew through Hong Kong in transit and decided to extend the stay for a few days to see me. Both of us were figuring out whether there was something between us. I was weird enough to not think of the age difference as being a major issue, but rather the fact that I had just started a new job that required me to be based in Hong Kong and he was a traveling yogi. I told you my life was all about my work.

We suddenly heard people yelling. A crowd started gathering around a little grocery stall on the street. As we walked toward the crowd, I realized there were three students doing a street survey. They all had their heads held low as the shopkeeper shouted at them and gathered other shopkeepers to surround them and condemn them for being involved in a protest that was going on at the time and being "bad for business."

I guess Peter had no idea what was going on, as all of the yelling was in Cantonese. Most of the bystanders were just shocked at what was unfolding, and many were still trying to make sense of what was happening.

I ran into the crowd and took one of the students in my arms. She started sobbing as I hugged her. I found myself trying to diffuse the situation, arguing back on behalf of the students because if there is one thing in the world I can't stand, it's someone being silenced and not having a chance to fight back. Other bystanders started to speak up. The shopkeepers no longer had the upper hand and stopped yelling.

You'll have to ask Peter for his side of the story, but in my mind, that was the moment he fell in love with me—that shift from a fondness to helplessly falling. I know that was the moment when I helplessly fell into love, too.

As my whole body was buzzing and shaking in agitation because of what had just happened and the political struggle that had led up to it, Peter simply said, "I'm proud of you."

I knew he had my back in that situation, but I also knew he was the rock I could count on to ground me so I wouldn't let my anger go overboard and do anything I would later regret. Maybe I reminded him of that guy he once was who tied himself to a ship in an anti-whaling protest. From my perspective, he was an inspiration for me to evolve and truly turn this changing-the-world thing into my life's work.

## LETTING GO 2.0

So my pursuit of hippiness began; the deep process of letting go of my first-phase-of-life baggage began.

Richard Rohr wrote in *Falling Upward* (2011) that as we move into the second phase of life, "we are very often at odds with our natural family and the 'dominant consciousness' of our cultures." Rohr, being a Catholic priest, went as far as this: "Jesus pulls no punches, saying you must 'hate' your home base in some way and make choices beyond it."

What does that sound like to you? Counterculture—like what a hippie would say, right?

I started more than two years of traveling with Peter in many more of the yoga teacher trainings, intensive workshops, and yoga retreats he taught around the world. I learned from Peter and from every other amazing person I met. I saw he held spaces for opportunities for growth and brought out the elevated version of many—including me.

The hippies I met and hung out with were primarily spiritual seekers who deliberately renounced mainstream society and materialistic pursuits to attain wisdom and enlightenment.

The biggest cultural shock was when I first gave the nomadic yoga-teaching and studying lifestyle a try on the island of Koh Phangan in Thailand. We were living at a retreat center literally named The Sanctuary nestled in the remote jungle of Haad Tien Bay.

I arrived with what must have been one of the biggest pieces of luggage the islanders had ever seen—as in no sensible person would have brought that. What took me to Haad Tien Bay was a "taxi boat," you see. Why "taxi"? I guess it was because the boat was, at most, the size of a taxi. I didn't get on or off it at a pier. It's the kind of taxi you had to walk into the water at a beach to get onto, and multiple people had to push it off the beach into the sea. I hope I've painted a clear picture in your head. Now add me with a piece of check-in-size luggage. It was quite embarrassing and out of place, really.

I might as well have had "high maintenance" tattooed on my forehead. But for me, that was already a huge downsizing exercise. I was going to live out of one piece of luggage for a few months; whatever I could pack in there was all I had. Not too long ago, I had been a shopaholic with a walk-in closet who wore different outfits to work every day and paraded that season's limited-edition Louis Vuitton and the most ridiculous heels by Christian Louboutin.

After quitting, I knew I would have to live for god knows how long on my savings while I tried to figure out what was next. My options, including how long I could stay in transition and whether I needed to spend some time making a living while in transition, depended on how much I *needed* for basic survival. The lower that amount, the more freedom I would have and for longer.

I sold, donated, and cleaned out about half of my stuff— accessories, garments, bags, shoes, home décor, CDs, books, and appliances. What was left was moved back to my parents' place to store and off I flew with my one suitcase.

Giving up the brand labels was easier than I thought; Louis Vuitton and Jimmy Choo would look extremely in appropriate on a jungle beach.

Giving up the job labels was a lot more difficult, but a hippie community was the best place to start doing it. There, nobody cared much about what anyone did for a living. Some people were living at the bay all year; some were regulars like the gelato business owner who typically spent summers in Italy and the rest of the year in Thailand; some people like Peter came here for three months or so every year to work as well as play. People didn't identify or pigeonhole each other primarily based on job titles. It was more like, "Tom hangs out on the smaller beach over the hill; Daisy is the one leading the dance circle tonight; ask Sebastian if you want to go paddling; Meera is staying here to write a book too."

I was staying in a modest but sufficient hut in the jungle: running water, yes; hot water, no; toilet flush system, no—or yes, if you count me holding a bucket of water and manually "flushing" as a system.

I freaked out in the beginning, but days went by and I started to appreciate the lesson.

Living in a less urban environment forced me to discern and prioritize what was it that I absolutely needed versus what I just wanted. Through living it, I understood that having running water in the house made a big difference to my standard of living—a toilet flushing system, less so—but having a toilet within the house, as a woman, did make a difference to living standards as well as safety level. Living the jungle island life made me more aware of the things I took for granted and the little nuances I autopiloted through. Enhanced awareness provided an opportunity to reconsider, reassess, and make conscious decisions about what was right for me instead of simply accepting and applying the norm as the default.

I let go of the stuff I owned, the label and identity I carried, and the living standard and amenities I was used to.

Still, those are but outer layers.

## FAILING AT LETTING GO 3.0

When you consciously go off the grid, you choose to not have society's collective construct as your safety net. One primary lure of the collective is the sense of security and belonging it provides for its followers. That's why it requires a lot of inner work to move beyond what Rohr called "family-of-origin stuff, local church stuff, cultural stuff, flag-and-country stuff" to find our own soul and destiny beyond what our parents and society want us to be.

On that path of moving beyond, you need something to replace that safety net promised by the collective. It boils down to the belief that the universe has your back. My faith in something bigger than me out there having my back goes up and down depending on the day or even the hour. Whether you call it God, angels, the Higher Self, it doesn't really matter; I usually use "universe" because of its inclusivity.

It's more natural for me to strive (and quite often thrive) at controlling instead of having faith, which requires surrendering.

Just the word "surrender" used to (and still does) trigger me.

That is letting go 3.0 and it is learned through experience. It has to be learned through the messiness of the world, not in a jungle beach sanctuary alone sitting in a perfect lotus pose.

That is probably the best way to explain why my pursuit of hippiness eventually came to an end.

Every day, Peter tried to convince me to do nothing and take care of myself first instead of jumping right into the next thing and the old patterns of being productive for the sake of it.

But I was not ready to renounce. I was still reactive.

Sure I was ridden with depression, swinging between complete dissociation due to a profound feeling of powerlessness and heart-wrenching pain and sadness because of all the wrongs I saw in the world. But I didn't see the pursuit of happiness to be the key out of my misery. I believed I was depressed because I had no purpose in life and I would be free from depression once I found my purpose and meaning. I couldn't see doing yoga and meditating to heal myself as a worthwhile goal in life when there were so many problems happening around us, from animal suffering to climate change.

The story of another Peter—Peter Barton, who founded a publicly traded media corporation—kept ringing in my head. When he was dying from cancer and looking back at his life, this is what he thought of his fellow MBA candidates:

"Bottom line: they were extremely bright people who would never really *do* anything, would never add much to society, would leave no legacy behind" (Shames, 2004).

Barton found this waste of potential terribly saddening.

I felt the same way looking at myself and many of my peers. This huge group of talented people running around the trading floors, board rooms, and around the globe doing what? Making the rich richer and climbing up the social ladder while we were at it?

I saw with my own eyes how Peter changed people's lives. I was so proud of him for touching so many people's hearts.

But I wanted to change the world in a big way. I wanted to unravel systemic problems. I wanted to create paradigm shifts.

I was gutted that I had already wasted so much of my working life "never really doing anything" of value. How could I do *nothing* and take care of myself first? I couldn't afford to waste even more time.

While Peter was mostly grounded and calm through the ups and downs of his life, including business and health issues, I was restless and agitated, bringing drama with me wherever we went.

We traveled to and lived in many of the most spiritual places in the world, from the jungle beach in Thailand to the spiritual capital Ubud in Bali, to secluded retreat centers in Sweden, to the Greek Islands and more. Beyond the beauty of nature and the gratitude I should have had for that dream life I was living, all I could see was social injustice and animal welfare problems happening everywhere I went.

One time when I should have been assisting Peter in the yoga teacher training, I ran off for days after finding a stray dog lurking around at different spots in the jungle in Thailand. I tracked down the history of where she had come from. Apparently, some drunk, idiotic tourists thought it'd be funny to take her on the taxi boat from the main island to the jungle and left her there. "Snowy" was a stray on the main island and had been taken care of by an animal rescue center. She had a long list of diseases, couldn't hold her bladder, and looked so thin.

Then my mission became to figure out a way to get her home and get the treatments she needed. Two kind English women and I formed a kind of rescue team and spent days befriending Snowy so she would get on a truck with us that would take us across the mountain back to the animal rescue center we would entrust her with. The "road," which didn't exist, was so rocky and bumpy that we had to hold on for dear life. We had to do the same with Snowy to avoid being thrown off the truck—which, of course, did not even have a proper door. Mission accomplished. Then things like this kept happening over and over again, like the time when I wanted to jump off Peter's scooter as we passed by a bare field and I saw a dog that was nothing but skin and bone.

Everywhere I went, I noticed these gigantic problems. I knew if I allowed myself to get sucked in, that would be it. I would be completely consumed, and soon enough, I'd be fostering thirty dogs and cats at a little villa overlooking the rice paddy in Bali, feeding them and cleaning up shit as my full-time job.

People told me the crime rate was going up in Bali because of the cheap labor coming from all around Indonesia. Well, what did they expect when these people were hired to build all these grand villas and yoga studios as white tourists and expatriates gentrified these Balinese villages and these workers were so poor they had to live and sleep in the construction sites where they worked? This is not to undermine the many expatriates I knew who were trying to give back to the community and create great job opportunities for the locals, but I found it very hard to live among very blatant injustice and suffering happening right in front of my eyes on a daily basis.

This is why I've only been to India once and never went back; this is also why people who really emerge themselves in India attain so much spiritual growth.

I was not, and still am not, spiritually mature. I reacted; I didn't want to surrender. I could not accept most things in life. Instead, I vowed to do whatever little bit I could to change them.

## SEASONS IN LIFE

There are lessons I haven't learned yet.

On the contrary, Peter was beyond the days when he had tied himself to a ship in an anti-whaling protest. He had once been an activist and a hippie; but there are seasons in life, and in the later stage, he was the older and wiser teacher, holding space for others fighting on the frontlines and creating sanctuary for them to retreat and mend their hearts—like how he had held space and provided sanctuary for me.

I was in another season. I had to go back out there and put myself through this journey. There's no skipping through what was coming and what I had to learn.

As most love stories go, often the reason that attracted you to someone ends up being the same thing that drives you apart.

By the end of our relationship, I realized I had become a burden to Peter's onward journey to go deeper spiritually and become one with the universe. Peter once mentioned his wish for his final days was to disappear into the Himalayan mountains where his life would end in solitude and peace. No fuss and traditions that belong to the physical world and human society—he would re-enter the circle of life and the embrace of Mother Earth quietly. I didn't trust I had it in me to let go of a man I loved without bringing in a crazy amount of drama.

The reality was that his days were more valuable than mine because, presumably, he had fewer of them remaining. I had to let him get on with the life lessons he was put in this world for as I went on with mine.

Peter used to say this in almost every class, "No judgment; no expectation; no comparison."

That deep reconciliation, that grace and serenity, will probably take a lifetime, but I did learn more about the meaning behind those words through the most fascinating unfolding of life events in this second phase of life.

After opening my heart, letting go of many first-phase-of-life labels and beliefs, and surrendering more deeply into this experience of falling upward, I re-engaged with the capitalistic reality.

I thought I was ready to make a difference in the world.

The question was, how?

## CHAPTER 5

# THE MANY FACETS OF ENTREPRENEURSHIP

———

*"Entrepreneurship is a career path—typically with iterations between established companies, your own startups, and the startups of others."*

−PROFESSOR BENJAMIN HALLEN

After quitting their corporate careers, many people naturally fall into entrepreneurial pursuits. A 2019 study showed 60 percent of people who start their own businesses are between the ages of forty and sixty (Guidant Financial, 2019). It seems logical. After all, if the kind of job you want doesn't exist, you create one for yourself. Well, you might want to brace yourself for a more confusing mishmash than the hippie jungle.

Welcome to the world of entrepreneurship. You've been warned.

While leaving my legal career had shaken my sense of identity to the core, it was the thought of being an entrepreneur (and being referred to as an entrepreneur on and off) that really created my identity crisis.

Many corporate professionals are used to being *qualified* for something and endorsed by some *recognized* organizations of such qualification. It felt like a lie calling myself an entrepreneur, which can mean anything or nothing. It's not a lie to call yourself a lawyer if you're qualified or call yourself a doctor if you're certified; the same goes for engineers, social workers, firefighters, or real estate agents. There is some sort of legal or industry standard you have to pass before you can call yourself a teacher, midwife, or blacksmith.

But what is the qualification for an entrepreneur? It's like calling yourself a writer, painter, or runner—there is zero entry barrier. That was a huge trigger to my imposter syndrome.

In hindsight, getting a master of entrepreneurship degree was my attempt to not be—or to not feel like—a complete fraud. From ideation to competitive strategy, business plan creation to leadership skills, accounting, finance, marketing, and legal stuff, I learned the essentials and passed the exam. I was stuck inside and outside of the classroom over twelve months with twenty-five peers and numerous mentors, partners, and communities with everybody calling themselves an entrepreneur. The funny thing is when I graduated, I still had no idea what an entrepreneur was, because an entrepreneur is not just one thing.

Instead of calling myself an entrepreneur, I started referring to myself as unemployed. At least that description was factually impeccable.

Here's my journey toward unemployment—or freedom from employment, depending on which camp you are in.

## FROM BALI TO SEATTLE

My entrepreneurial journey began in Bali. This mystical island in the Indian Ocean was once a spiritual hub visited by seekers, surfers, and burnouts. Nowadays, Bali is also a vibrant tech startup hub. The "digital nomads" in Bali shaped my original understanding of what it is to be entrepreneurial.

Since many of them are corporate escapees and have chosen to restart in an island paradise, these people are not only trying to start a business, but also to re-invent their lives in a holistic way. They are challenging the status quo of what work looks like. Bootstrapping to building their own businesses while striking a work-life balance seems to be the goal. Chris Guillebeau's *The $100 Startup* (2012) and Tim Ferriss's *The 4-Hour Work Week* (2005) were the bibles that set the road map of how to be this new breed of successful entrepreneur. One thing that didn't resonate with me so well, as you can tell from the titles of these books, is there's an over-representation of "hackers"—people trying to hack life: do less, get more.

I was living that life and blending in for a while. Looking back, we were so ahead of our time. The world has now caught up on working from home, while years ago I was already living not only a work-from-home but also a work-from-beach lifestyle. We were not just working remotely but being location independent. Wherever there was a laptop and a Wi-Fi connection, I had a virtual office. There were no geographical boundaries—thus, the term "digital nomads."

On a typical day, I would either be writing a blog on a beach while sipping on a coconut or emailing my virtual assistant at a "hot desk" in a hipster co-working space looking over a rice paddy. I signed up for all sorts of online classes to learn about ideal client avatars, creating websites, email marketing, and Facebook ads. You see, my first business idea was to help corporate professionals like myself quit the rat race and live a more purpose-driven life. I wrote an e-book to build a following, created YouTube videos, and almost got myself on a TEDx stage.

According to the expert industry formula, the next thing to do was to launch my online course and start charging for it. Everyone thought I wanted to be a coach; I didn't. I was as lost as everyone else, if not more. I had no interest in helping anyone who wanted to explore career change just because they "work in a toxic environment" or wanted to be their own boss and "work on their own terms" instead. I was interested in exploring what I call the Mission circle, and help others contribute to "what the world needs" as part of their career change—not just the intersection of Talent, Passion, and Market.

My second business was a step closer to my mission to alleviate animal suffering: what I would pitch as the "vegan Sephora." The idea was to be a one-stop shop for great skincare and cosmetic brands that did not engage in animal testing. Although the world had started to ban animal testing for cosmetics, a law requiring animal testing on beauty products sold in China meant in reality, most of the notable global brands were still engaging in animal testing (Lim, 2021). Giving up on the Chinese consumer market was not really an option from a pure profit perspective. With my business, I wanted to frame and demonstrate ending animal testing as a business opportunity to assist the existing social movements. I thought engaging with policymakers as a (successful) business owner and stakeholder would be more effective than engaging as an activist. I was naïve. It was not a conventional intention to start a business, but it set the scene for what was to come for me.

By the time I moved to Seattle, I had put aside my first business and my second business was not gaining as much traction as I had hoped. Desperately trying to make it work, I ended up enrolling in that master's program on entrepreneurship I mentioned. It was essentially a company incubator in a campus setting. I wanted to learn the essentials and gain the network to turn my business around.

From the Land of Gods to the home of tech startups-turned-giants like Amazon, Bali and Seattle were night and day. In Bali, almost everyone in two startup founders are hippies consumed by wanderlust; in Seattle, there's about a 50 percent chance the person you just met works for Amazon or Microsoft (or has sold their business to Amazon or Microsoft) and has ambition to create the next Uber or Netflix.

I had gotten sick of traditional Balinese coffee. Hot water and the fine grind coffee are mixed directly in the cup and the grind never quite dissolves fully. The brown, muddy mass always left at the bottom of the cup is like my unfinished first business: an eyesore that kept reminding me of the money and effort wasted.

I was then in a very different city of coffee where the most successful coffee venture in history, Starbucks, was born. Seattle was more the kind of hub to scale one's business up.

## THE PURPOSE DELUSION

The most classic academic definition of entrepreneurship used by Harvard Business School and beyond is entrepreneurship is the pursuit of opportunity beyond resources controlled (Einsenmann, 2013). Breaking it down intuitively, "pursuit" implies a quest for something and taking action, "opportunity" implies novelty and possibility, and "beyond resources controlled" implies not letting current circumstances limit your dreams and imagination. Sure, I am a sucker for all the above. Maybe I am an entrepreneur.

With this definition, Martin Luther King and Mother Teresa are certainly entrepreneurs; so are nonprofit founders like Premal Shah, who created Kiva to alleviate poverty through innovative crowdfunded microlending. And who is to say J. K. Rowling is not an entrepreneur? She pursued the idea of Harry Potter and turned it into a reality while being a single mom on state benefits.

All of them pursued something novel. They pushed boundaries, changed the rules of the game, created something completely new and original, disrupted industries—if not the entire world—and shifted cultures and mindsets beyond the resources they had and against all odds. I certainly aspire to be all that and have been undertaking many such projects (although with much humbler impact) over the years. Identifying myself as an entrepreneur seems right.

Much confusion (and frustration) cropped up, however, when I realized the societal expectations I tried so hard to set myself free from were grabbing hold of me again.

In the Seattle startup scene, as an entrepreneur, apparently I must want to get venture capital funding someday; I must want an exit through IPO or being acquired; I must want to be a founder or CEO and, of course, a unicorn. If you only read about entrepreneurship from *Techcrunch* and *Fast Company*, apparently this is what makes you an entrepreneur: you are hardwired to want to grow as fast as possible, scale as big as possible, and raise as much funding as possible—faster, bigger, richer, exit, and repeat.

For quite some time, I thought there was something wrong with me, because, with all due respect, that sounds like hell. The Seattle-born Starbucks is still not my cup of coffee.

If I became an entrepreneur to fulfill my "why," was my business really fulfilling that search for a reason of being?

After experiencing two extremes on the spectrum of the startup environment, this is what I learned: I needed to find out for myself what kind of entrepreneur I am. That self-discovery is probably the most truly entrepreneurial part of the journey of starting a business.

## BACK TO IDEATION

Faced with confusion in the direction of my entrepreneurial endeavors and the fourth anniversary of my melodramatic declaration to quit my high-fly legal career to "find my purpose," I had nothing much to show for my decision except proven failures and consuming self-doubt. I was ashamed I had let down my family and friends whose opinion toward my life decisions ranged from being supportive but worried I was throwing my life away to outright disappointment that led them to give up on me.

I ran away from wet and chilly Seattle. I ran away from those people talking about go-to-market strategy, revenue models, pivoting, competition, getting funded, scaling, and exiting. I retreated from judging and feeling judged for calling myself an entrepreneur.

I surrendered and emerged into a weeklong conscious dancing workshop in what has since become one of my soul homes: the Esalen Institute in Big Sur, California. As I experienced the movement meditation practice with a room of strangers, the universe showed me the way out of my struggle to balance the four circles (Passion, Mission, Talent, and Market) through four messengers in the most enchanted way.

Day one: I met a fellow dancer who was an anesthesiologist working in Silicon Valley. "When you're surrounded by all those startup people, they make it sound like it's *the* thing to do. They talk about making a difference, changing the world...but in the end, they only care about the money and want Google to buy them out," he said. He had also been thinking about starting his own business and had taken a course on entrepreneurship at Stanford University. "I came from New York, and at least those folks own up to their own shit," he said.

The universe tried to get on my good side by showing me someone who completely agreed with my point of view. Good job. I was listening!

Day two: In came my roommate, a venture capitalist from Palo Alto, as I was saying that entrepreneurs are just the same creatures as big corporates, except they are not yet big or successful and are more desperate. She was surprised by how anti-startup I sounded.

"Sure, that's true for 70 to 80 percent of them, but there are also some good ones out there. I have worked with a software startup that helps cancer patients and another that's educational," she said.

A different perspective. My judgments were triggered, but what she said made me realize that I judged because I felt judged. I assumed people like her would judge me for throwing my "bright future" away for some stupid, idealistic notion of life, and I tried to protect myself by judging her and "her people." She might have also felt judged by me, as I was being self-righteous and despising her for her "mainstream success."

Day three: The universe showed me my past and reminded me of the progress I had made.

"We do the thing, get the money—my work is *empty*! I don't feel like I'm doing any good, helping anybody..." This might as well have been me from four years ago talking. In front of me was someone who worked at a private equity firm to feed his body, created a blog and podcast on the side to feed his soul, and struggled to find a way to leave the private equity firm for good by generating income from his podcast.

This was exactly me four years ago.

Day four: The universe showed me what kind of future was possible. Another fellow dancer shared about her move to San Francisco after the dance retreat to start a new job. "It's very new. A business accelerator for ventures that use the nonprofit model or where the bottom line is measured only by impact!"

Thank you, Universe. I learned enough to make the decision to close my second business for good.

The truth is, I was spending most of my time and energy on survival—the survival of my business in its infancy. I was impatient. My intention was to have an impact, but reality looked like I'd be spending the next five years on survival before I could even start thinking about making an impact.

The truth is, I was frustrated with the people around me. They all said they were trying to make a difference and change the world, but then I looked at their business plans and I couldn't help but ask, "What differences are you making and how are you changing the world?"

It was not anyone's fault. This is the harsh reality. It doesn't matter whether you are searching for a job or building a business. There is a reason why we all start with the first-phase-of-life type of work and why the TM (Talent-Market) combo is typically the default choice. First, you need to survive financially, whether as an employee or a business owner. Then we have the "luxury" to add Passion to the mix. Usually after that, we have the "privilege" to consider Mission. This is the progression into the second phase of life, which also applies to a business. A startup is no doubt still in its first phase of life.

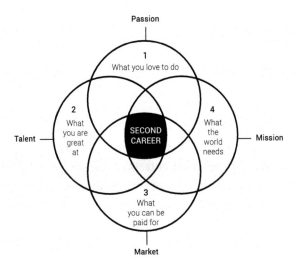

In Bali, the startup community was led by Circle 1 (Passion): the passion for travel and the freedom that comes with location independence. The "digital nomad" model primarily takes advantage of living in a country with a much lower living standard compared with metropolitan areas to buy more time to grow the company and get access to more affordable human resources. In that way, it allows less waiting to be put on Circle 3 (Market) and prioritizes Passion instead.

In Seattle, I was pulled back to my old life. It was more focused on the intersection of Circle 2 (Talent) and Circle 3 (Market), as most conventional career paths are. Yes, with an innovation twist, but fundamentally not that different.

There was still no Circle 4: a focus (or at least equal weighting) on **Mission**.

In true entrepreneurial style, I went through many pivots and iterations. They all happened for a reason. Little did I know I was getting prepared for what I then stumbled upon: nonprofit entrepreneurship.

## NONPROFIT ENTREPRENEURSHIP

I had no idea entrepreneurship could be about anything other than making profit. Isn't entrepreneurship all about starting a business in the hopes of generating a profit? Nonprofit entrepreneurship? Now that's disruption of the status quo.

After many twists and turns, I found people who talked like this:

"I built up my career following life's path. You know, I worked really hard in school, got the grades, graduated early, got my master's degree, got a good job, and made good money. But I always knew that I wanted to be a changemaker," said Christine Gould, the founder and CEO of Thought For Food (TFF). "And I knew that I would somehow be a changemaker in the food and agriculture space. They say when you find your purpose, life makes sense. Like, you look back and everything looks like a piece of the puzzle. It makes so much sense that I founded TFF. It's literally everything that I believe in and love to do."

Christine had that spark of passion in her eyes that was highly contagious. "From innovation to community-building to collaborating with unconventional partners, I've even been able to weave in my love for DJ-ing and dancing in a way that makes total sense for what we do. The best part is that TFF is really needed in the world. It's helping to solve one of the biggest challenges facing our planet by bringing new minds and new approaches from every part of the world. It is my purpose," said Christine with a big grin.

It took me years to learn how to discern who *my kind of people* are. Nothing illustrates it better than in the first conversation Christine and I had. Halfway through, Christine was already saying, "We are the same person." And I thought, "Yes, same-same indeed!"

Note the keywords. Instead of "I want to leave my nine-to-five," "I want to be my own boss," or "I'd like to make money doing what I love most," these people talk about finding their *purpose*; it's not about whether the *market wants* this, but whether the *world needs* this.

It may seem a subtle (and sometimes debatable) difference, but in my mind, there is a clear distinction between a company simply minimizing or compensating for the negative impact inevitably created by its business and one with changemaking baked into its core business strategies. The former usually makes efforts in fulfilling its corporate social responsibilities (CSR), which is important and can be very impactful too, but the latter is fundamentally changing the way of delivering a product or service to mitigate or eliminate something negative in the world.

An example may be a chicken egg producer increasing the size of cage to adhere to higher animal welfare standards and better manage the risk of animal-borne diseases versus a plant-based egg producer creating animal-egg substitutes made completely from plants, thereby eliminating the need for industrial animal farming as part of the production process. The latter are my people. I had been lost, and now I might have found my tribe.

Christine started TFF as a side project in 2011 when she was still working at Syngenta, a global agribusiness company in Switzerland. TFF was built to be an innovation platform for sustainable food and agriculture. To date, TFF's programs have helped more than thirty thousand innovators from more than 175 countries generate thousands of viable business plans and have successfully launched more than sixty new food and agriculture-related startups that have collectively raised over two hundred million dollars. Its flagship event, the TFF Global Challenge, shakes up the traditionally quite conservative agricultural sector with a showcase of next-gen perspectives and solutions from around the world, art installations, and speakers from business, policy, tech, and creative industries (TFF, 2021).

Light sparkled in her eyes as Christine recalled the first-ever TFF Global Challenge and TFF Summit. "I was on maternity leave. My child was seven weeks old, and I remember bringing him on stage at the event and nursing him backstage. It was a truly special atmosphere. My parents and husband were there. There was no hierarchy or sense of pretense that you find at other corporate events. It was all very authentic, very energizing, and people say it was the best event of their lives because of that." Approaching the tenth anniversary of TFF, it has not always been an easy road. After quitting her corporate job while having a family with two young children depending on her, she had a few years of zero income from TFF and had to fill that gap by doing side hustles.

So why nonprofit?

"I'm a person who's very intrinsically motivated by purpose and impact," Christine explained. "I think business, especially entrepreneurship, as it's always been done is about 'how to monetize.' But I like thinking first: what is the right thing to do? How do I do this in the best way possible that can help more people? Sometimes that's at odds with trying to make profit."

There are sacrifices and challenges, but being a nonprofit allows Christine to stay true to her vision. "We are engaging the next generation. We work with young people, the millennials and Gen Zs, who I believe are the most equipped generations the world has ever seen to solve these complex, systemic challenges we face. They are the largest, most diverse, entrepreneurially minded, purpose minded, and collaborative generation the world has ever seen. How do we unleash their potential? When you're dealing with young people all over the world, and a lot of our work is in, for example, Africa and Southeast Asia, they don't have access to the money and resources that other countries may have. Our program literally changes their lives because it's a free program that connects them to others and gives them the chance to shine on the global stage." Innovators, including students, can join TFF's competitions and events for free to build their businesses with support and mentorship from its platform, get connected with industry partners, and win prizes to kick-start their ideas.

Christine is essentially running an accelerator, but her mission requires her not to be bound by a traditional for-profit accelerator business model. "We help the next generation of entrepreneurs stay true to what they want to do, which is impact so they can put it at the core of their startups. We empower them to do that by giving them networking capabilities and other support so that they don't feel like they have to sell out for the profit. That's different from how existing business has been led." Not running a conventional accelerator model also means TFF helps incubate nonprofit startups as well as for-profit startups depending on what business vehicle and model serves the end purpose.

An example is reNature, a startup in regenerative agroforestry. There are not many for-profit companies out there dealing with agroforestry because it has a very long-time horizon; reNature established itself as a nonprofit first. After building a track record and having some success, according to Christine, the startup is now building a for-profit arm because it is starting to attract bigger companies building their stories around sustainability (reNature, 2021).

"I think there is something really special and unique about the next generation. They want to build businesses that have impact at the core." The spark in Christine's eyes again lit up her screen as she was conducting a video call with me while jammed in the bottom bunk of her seven-year-old son's bed.

My own eyes lit up when Christine said, "It's a very interesting crowd we have at TFF. We're not hippies, but we have hippies; we're not cutthroat entrepreneurs, but we have some of those. We're different."

I saw Bali and Seattle coming together; the strong glue was Circle 4 (Mission).

This was neither Balinese coffee nor corporate Starbucks. I might have finally found my unique coffee blend.

It is about the intersection of the four circles; Mission had been that missing piece all along. Just like Albert, who had moved from engineering to fighting epidemics; Francis, who quit corporate to build a social enterprise platform; and, of course, Christine, who is fixing the broken food system through innovation, we all pursue one thing in common.

In my coffee blend, Mission has to be a key ingredient.

## CHAPTER 6

# DOING GOOD AS A CAREER

---

*"I cannot do all the good that the world needs.*
*But the world needs all the good that I can do."*

—JANA STANFIELD

The world is on fire.

With a video loop of the Amazon rainforest burning behind him, Dr. Pat Brown made the passionate appeal to career scientists at a press conference via Zoom (Poinski, 2020).

"Scientists and engineers, we want you. The most important scientific and engineering problem in human history. A great environment, great resources, great colleagues. You can't beat it, okay? Leave your stupid job and come join us."

Pat, a career scientist himself, founded Impossible Foods in 2011 when he was on sabbatical from being a biochemistry professor at Stanford University's medical school. He was in his fifties when he became an entrepreneur. In an interview in 2020, he said he wished he had had a better understanding of how catastrophic the use of animals in the food system was when he was in his twenties. Then, instead of going into biomedical research, he would have gone right to work on the problem of industrial animal agriculture (Eadicicco, 2020).

In 2019, Impossible Foods reached a valuation of two billion dollars. But to Pat, the key to starting a successful company had less to do with business-oriented goals and more to do with the problem a startup aims to solve.

"The main thing I would say to people who are entrepreneurial is pick a problem that matters to the world," said Pat. "If you think you have the capability of coming up with a useful solution to the problem, that's the big opportunity. I feel like the world does not need more gadgets to collect data on everyone, Alexa-enabled toothbrushes or whatever. Do something actually useful."

I think that deserves a mic drop. I'm going to create a meme if nobody else does.

All of those brainstorming sessions spent in and before business school, when I participated in startup generation events and competitions, the focus was always in coming up with startup ideas addressing "unmet needs" and "pain points" of customers. With all due respect—or not—fuck the lot of them.

Now I understand why they all left me feeling empty inside.

I don't care how many unmet needs there are for the people who want to have an Alexa-enabled toothbrush. What about what the world actually needs? What about doing something useful?

## EFFECTIVE ALTRUISM

What frustrated me a lot in the purpose rabbit hole was that too many people tossed around phrases like "make a difference" with a very low bar of what "making a difference" actually meant. They had the best intention to do good but were not equipped to take trackable actions that generate measurable results.

Startups do have a tendency to make themselves out as heroes that will save the world. Then you look at their business plans and experience the ultimate anticlimax when you learn that they're just making Alexa-enabled toothbrushes.

"That's lying!" I spent years being bitter and complaining about startup culture to anyone who would listen.

"Nobody's lying to you," others would say. "People can interpret 'making a difference' in many ways, and making a small difference is still making a difference."

"If I ever claim that I'm good at something, I have to be *really* good—like at least be in the ninetieth percentile. Otherwise, I shouldn't be shamelessly claiming I'm good at all. If someone claims they are making a difference, I'm being led to believe they are at least making a *significant* difference," I'd argue.

"Well, you can't blame others for you being so idealistic and borderline delusional." Okay, point taken.

Fortunately, other than the meme I'm going to create, there is more guidance on *how* we can put Pat's advice into action.

Starting in the late 2000s by organizations like Giving What We Can and GiveWell, effective altruism (EA) is a philosophy and social movement that uses evidence and reason to determine the most effective ways to do good and make the world a better place.

The key is to aim a little higher and ask a little more of oneself. While no system is perfect, EA provides a good framework for some solid, no-bullshit self-evaluation and critical assessment of what it takes to not shamelessly claim you are making a difference.

EA starts with the recognition that most of us want to make a difference. We see suffering, injustice, and death and are moved to do something about them. But the key is working out what that "something" is. There are two parts to the question: what are the problems and what are the solutions. EA's response is to be extremely data-driven and research-focused and use careful reasoning to work out how to help others as much as possible.

The goal is to move people to focus their efforts on the *most promising* solutions to the world's *most pressing* problems. With this combination, it's not just altruism but effective altruism.

One of EA's most intriguing—and to a certain extent, most controversial—aspects is it starts with telling you what the problems are that you ought to solve first in order to leave this world a better place. It can seem a little counterintuitive at first, but upon deeper reflection, this truly takes the ego out of the equation. Doing good should have nothing to do with just making you feel a little better about yourself. According to the EA philosophy, if we choose a cause that simply happens to be salient to us, we may overlook the most important problems of our time.

Working on a cause is likely to be highly impactful to the extent that the cause is:

- Great in *scale:* It affects many lives by a great amount.

- Highly *neglected:* Few other people are working on addressing the problem.

- Highly *solvable* or *tractable:* Additional resources will do a great deal to address it.

On the basis of this reasoning, the three most pressing issues for humanity are: extreme poverty, animal suffering, and "long-term future." Long-term future issues are basically the minimization of global catastrophic risks, also known as existential risks, including climate change and hostile artificial intelligence (Effective Altruism, 2021).

Once you have identified the *most pressing* problems, you can then move on to figure out what may be the *most promising* solutions. Most altruistic interventions have proven to be very low impact. Remember Albert from chapter two? His first mission-oriented career move took him to South Africa to work on the AIDS epidemic. According to a 2013 study by Dr. Toby Ord, different types of intervention can generate miles apart impact in reducing the spread of HIV and AIDS: Using the number of years of healthy life that can be saved as measuring unit, the best strategy (educating high-risk groups) is estimated to be 1,400 times more impactful than the worst strategy (surgical treatment). Educating high-risk groups is also about twice as effective as the second-best strategy, which is condom distribution.

How can we find and work on the *most promising* solutions? Albert went through a few pivots after returning to Canada from South Africa. In 2013, he joined Dr. Kamran Khan, a practicing infectious disease physician and professor of medicine with the Division of Infectious Diseases at the University of Toronto, in a digital health startup BlueDot. BlueDot has developed global early warning technology for infectious diseases. It tracks over 150 infectious diseases around the clock and anticipates their spread and impact to empower national and international agencies to better anticipate and respond to emerging threats.

"During the four, five years there I came across so many epidemics—H7N1, H9N1, Ebola—and BlueDot is now heavily involved in COVID-19 internationally," said Albert. BlueDot uses an AI-driven algorithm. As Dr. Khan said, "Governments may not be relied upon to provide information in a timely fashion." BlueDot was among the first in the world to identify the emerging risk from COVID-19 and deliver insights worldwide to mobilize responses to the pandemic.

It correctly predicted the virus would jump from Wuhan in China to Bangkok, Seoul, Taipei, and Tokyo in the days following its initial appearance (Niller, 2020).

"We build a forewarning system, but the reality of the situation is human nature is often reactive and not proactive," said Albert. In search of an even more promising solution to another most pressing problem, Albert has since made a further move. Now the co-founder of impact investing firm Dao Foods, Albert is tackling the issue of industrial animal agriculture like Dr. Pat Brown.

Industrial animal farming is one of the rare industries that checks all three categories EA research has identified as the most pressing problems in the world. It is one of the biggest culprits of climate change, which is one of the biggest existential risks identified by EA (Weathers and Hermanns, 2017); a direct cause of animal suffering and extreme poverty. The United Nations World Food Council estimates transferring 10 to 15 percent of cereals fed to livestock to humans is enough to raise the world's food supply to feed the current population (Turner, 2018). Since COVID-19, there has been increased awareness of another existential risk that industrial animal agriculture poses. In July 2020, a joint International Livestock Research Institute and UNEP report based on research from dozens of scientists spanning the globe came to one conclusion: the way we interact with and consume animals is the main driver increasing the prevalence of zoonotic disease. The "human-mediated factors" behind the emergence of pandemics, as listed in the report, included increasing human demand for animal protein, unsustainable agricultural intensification, and increased use and exploitation of wildlife. In other words, it's safe to say our desire for meat and other animal products will most likely be responsible for the next pandemic (Borrud and King, 2020).

Albert's firm is one of the very first players in the Chinese alternative protein scene, backing thirty startups that focus on the Chinese plant-based protein market.

"What excites me is that we can go to the source of the problem. It's no longer just philanthropy and social enterprise; this is a real opportunity to activate business models and move capital to solve this global problem."

Just like Pat, Albert believes in better alternatives being the *most promising* solution. "We're not going to solve the problem by declaring war on the incumbent industry or telling people to change their diets," Brown said. "The only way to do it is by making products that do a better job of delivering what consumers value from meat and these other foods" (Feloni, 2019).

"This is an effective altruist's dream," said Albert. The trajectory has shown that the biggest and fastest-growing demand for meat has come from China for the past few decades (USDA, 2014). Albert is now working on bringing a *most promising* solution to a *most pressing* problem.

## A DIFFERENT KIND OF CAREER ADVICE

Many organizations have since grown out of the EA movement. One such organization is 80,000 Hours. It provides resources to help people lead high-impact careers. Whether you have strong quantitative skills, government and policy expertise, or a marketing, life sciences, or engineering background, 80,000 Hours has mapped out comprehensive priority career paths and suggestions for you.

Michelle Hutchinson, as the head of advising at 80,000 Hours, has given advice to literally hundreds of people seeking to pursue impact-led careers. She typically tries to get people to flip their framing from "What are a whole host of jobs that would do *some good?*" to "Which seems most appealing?" to considering "What things are the *most impactful?*", and finally, "Which might I be personally well suited for?"

Michelle primarily works with fresh graduates and people earlier on in their careers. The sky is the limit. According to Michelle, the result of this difference in framing is it primes them to go for those jobs hundreds of times more impactful than others.

To me, that framing is revolutionary and I wish I had learned it before I got stuck in the purpose rabbit role for years. The framing also works in a career change scenario to think through impact and evaluate opportunities.

Michelle shared a very common scenario of someone with a relatively good corporate job who would like to go into sustainability consulting or something that feels a little more rewarding to do more good. What Michelle would say (and actually has said) is, "Well, that does sound *a bit better* than a standard corporate job, but have you considered something really quite different?" Her rationale is twofold. First, sustainability consulting is already in the public consciousness.

It is less neglected compared with many other high-impact areas. Second, sustainability consulting typically focuses on helping one company get a bit more sustainable at the margin. It's not particularly likely to have high leverage as opposed to, for instance, influencing regulations all companies are required to follow.

The person who received this advice from Michelle is Ben Dixon. Ben was a UK qualified accountant with four years of experience as finance consultant in one of the big four firms who was considering his next steps.

In analyzing and concluding what his next career move should be, Ben's reasoning was aligned with Michelle's advice and heavily based on counterfactual analysis, as many EAs I know think about as well. The "counterfactual" measures what would have happened in the absence of a certain intervention compared with the estimated outcomes in the presence of such an intervention. This was how Ben's analysis went: in the case of sustainability consulting, there's an existing market where a company makes a call for bids to hire a consultant for its project. There is no shortage of sustainability consultants. Multiple consultancy firms would make their bids. The counterfactual of whether Ben's consultancy puts in a bid or not is simply whether he's in the running to get that project. If he didn't, someone else would.

Another consideration for Ben was that the sustainability consulting project might not produce the best positive impact overall. Ben's thought was while in many cases what is good for profits may also be good for the environment, the two don't always relate. This is sometimes called "greenwashing," which, in many projects, is the net positive impact may be very small because the fundamentals of the business itself are not changed. We have touched on this point earlier with the difference between a business *fundamentally solving* existing problems in the world versus efforts made to amend an existing business model to *reduce the bad* inevitable by-products from the fundamentals of a business.

Ben thinks people aiming to do good should consider working for charities and governments because they produce public goods that benefit society overall. "Public goods are what can be used by anyone—like clean water, hospitals, and research—but tend to be undersupplied," said Ben. "Businesses tend not to produce those because they have a profit motive." After quitting his finance consultancy job, Ben moved to work as the finance lead, overseeing a turnover of thirty million dollars for the Centre for Effective Altruism. The CEA freely provides public goods, including building a community of students and professionals that act on EA principles to bring change to the world.

This line of thinking, as one can see from the focus of 80,000 Hours, tends to lead to a bias for research, nonprofit work (or supporting nonprofit work through gifting and philanthropy), or going into the public sector. Is it impossible to find or create for-profit work with effective altruism at its core? It goes back to the fundamental conflict over which to prioritize: Market or Mission (Circle 3 or 4).

## TO PROFIT OR NOT TO PROFIT

Even though my "vegan Sephora" business failed, building a fundamentally mission-focused business is doable.

I still believe it's possible to build an effectively altruistic business. Maybe I'm idealistic and borderline delusional, but I need to believe it's not impossible to be both effectively altruistic and profitable.

Part of me is too jaded to have any faith we can change the world for the better by relying primarily on people being selfless and doing the right thing. We've had centuries of history to prove that has never worked—just being realistic. See? Maybe I'm not that idealistic and delusional after all.

In fact, companies like Impossible Foods are exactly the proof that creating an effectively altruistic business is possible. Both Pat Brown and Albert Tseng are trying to do the same thing: using the power of the market and business to solve one of the world's most pressing problems. In the case of Impossible Foods, these are the fundamentals of its business; the company's mission is to halt biodiversity collapse and reverse global warming by eliminating the need for animal agriculture. Its product uses 96 percent less land and 87 percent less water and produces 89 percent fewer greenhouse gas emissions compared with conventional beef from cows; it aims to replace livestock-based products. A 2020 market study found that 92 percent of Impossible Burger sales come directly at the expense of animal-derived meats (Fortuna, 2020). World Animal Protection estimates plant-based additions to fast food menus are saving 250,000 animals a year (Williamson, 2019).

This is one of the best examples of a company with EA baked into its core business strategy. Every additional dollar of sale the company makes demonstrates a direct causal link with additional positive impact and solutions to those most pressing problems including climate change and animal suffering.

Building a mission-focused business is much harder than creating a purely profit-driven company. But when it's done right, it's way more powerful—whether a person or business: same-same. Where P-M-T-M (Passion-Mission-Talent-Market) intersect, that's where the stars align and it's magical.

I'm fortunate enough to have seen it with my own eyes—not once but many times now—that this is not impossible! So yes, I believe.

Remember how, before I ran off to be a hippie, I was employee number twelve of a social startup?

That company, Green Monday, is another example of a star-aligned setup. To this day, Green Monday has the most genius business structure and strategy I've ever encountered. Green Monday is a master in staging. The staging of its corporate structure is even more fascinating than the staging of its product launches. Green Monday built the first arm under its group (a nonprofit) back in 2012 when alternative protein was not even a thing and the term "plant-based" had only started to emerge. The early 2010s was a defining watershed moment when vegetarianism and veganism were ripe for a complete rebranding to penetrate the mainstream market. Green Monday's advocacy arm created awareness, educated consumers, and from a pure business perspective, created the demand as well as the brand goodwill (Green Monday, 2021).

The second arm used to be distribution that sourced products to satisfy the demand created. Green Monday negotiated the distribution rights of products like Beyond Meat in 2014 and has been expanding the line of brands it carries ever since.

The third arm, venture capital, was what I was hired to create. Having a stake in the products the company distributes makes a lot of sense, and Green Monday was in effect the first and only marketing partner many plant-based brands relied on to build their customer base in Asia from scratch.

For-profit or not-for-profit? My experience at Green Monday taught me it's many times more powerful if you are both and more to create that P-M-T-M (Passion-Mission-Talent-Market) intersection and powerful synergy, individual or company, same-same.

Today, Green Monday is a heavyweight in the plant-based industry with its own grocery store chain, restaurant, plant-based meat startup, and venture capital fund, along with the nonprofit arm it began with almost ten years ago. Never in our wildest dreams could we have imagined from then to now growing into a company with over 400 staff members operating in over eight countries in Asia and is expanding into the UK and beyond. David and Francis, who co-founded Green Monday, were my very first mentors on this path less travelled.

Since Green Monday, you've seen me try multiple things and fall on my face more than a few times. A common theme was emerging though—I was only interested in dedicating my second career to freeing the oppressed from suffering. And out of the many oppressed beings in the world, I was passionate about freeing the animals. My entrepreneurial experiences had taught me I had no interest in (nor am I good at) first building something, spending years in a first-phase-in-life detour to survive and be successful, before I could create the actual altruistic impact.

I wanted to make a difference now. And that was when I stumbled upon the next exciting opportunity.

## CHAPTER 7

# THE DREAM GIG

——

*"There are just moments when all the stars
are aligned for breakthrough products."*

–JOHN SCULLY

Ladies and gentlemen, it's the moment we've been waiting for.

I landed my dream gig—finally.

Let's have a little recap of what has happened up to this point.
I tried to be a hippie; failed. I tried to become a full-time
yogini; failed. I tried to be an entrepreneur; failed, twice.
And then, finally, all the stars aligned.

## ALIGNING THE STARS

After all of these years, I now have a theory or two about how
to get the stars to align for you.

It's equal part sitting on your arse and not sitting on your arse.

When it happens, you'll know it. It will be so clear that without a doubt in your mind, you'll drop everything and go for it; however, it takes many "wrong" turns (although arguably, there are no *wrong* turns) and intensive self-discovery for us to get to that clarity. The universe is not going to waste a star alignment on you when you're not yet ready, because you wouldn't even realize it if its arse were sitting on your face.

That's the sitting-on-your-arse part. Be patient while waiting for the right timing because it's *all* about the timing.

The not-sitting-on-your-arse part: make sure you are learning and growing while you wait so once the opportunity appears, you're ready to seize it.

In my journey to get to my dream gig, my stepping stones were built through equal parts sitting and not sitting. I got the Green Monday job while sitting in a café; but I only got the job because I had been a vegetarian for a few years at that point, had a decade of legal experience, and was desperate enough to grab a stranger on the street and give an elevator pitch about myself. For the few years of trying to become a hippie, I sat and meditated a lot; but I also did yoga teacher trainings and learned many modalities to deep dive into self-awareness, discovery, and healing. As a digital nomad, I sat on beaches in Thailand and Bali and called them my office, most of those times with my butt in the sand, but I was also reading and learning all I could to create my next career.

In hindsight, it was a continuous pivoting and learning process to find out how I could get the four circles to intersect. When the four circles intersected, that's when the stars aligned!

To better illustrate this, let me score each job I had on the four circles of Talent, Money, Passion, and Mission, each circle out of a full score of 100.

My first career, from law school to the final fuck-it moment, lasted for fifteen years. These are the scores: Talent (90); Money (100); Passion (ten); and Mission (0).

The following five years after I quit, I've tried four things:

- Job at a plant-based social enterprise: Talent (70); Money (30); Passion (30); and Mission (80).

- Teach yoga: Talent (80); Money (0); Passion (50); and Mission (30).

- Writer or coaching business: Talent (80); Money (0); Passion (90); and Mission (30).

- Vegan e-commerce business: Talent (50); Money (10); Passion (50); and Mission (80).

And finally, the dream gig:

- Alternative proteins nonprofit: Talent (70); Money (30); Passion (70); and Mission (100).

If any of the circles are at zero, the stars are probably not aligned; having said that, each of us has a different *weighting* of the circles we seek at different phases of our lives. For instance, it would be way worse to have a low score on the Money circle in the first phase of our vocational life while we're trying to build up some safety net financially and still pay off student loans. To have a job that scores very low on Talent would also be quite disastrous in the first phase in life because you would not be able to hold down a job at all; whereas further along in your career path, you'd have enough experience and career assets to buy yourself more time and leeway to master something, even if it's a little outside of your born-talent zone.

It is therefore quite normal to find that in the early years of our careers, we have a skewed weighting toward Money and Talent; but as time goes by, it becomes less and less comfortable to have a zero score on Passion and Mission.

### GETTING THE DREAM JOB

The way I got my dream job was quite straight-forward, but let me back up a little and say simple doesn't mean easy.

Up to this point, we've been through a journey—through both my and others' stories—of unlearning, discerning, and letting go. With the things you no longer need out of the way, you've cleared up space to welcome what needs to happen and you are less likely to screw it up by being distracted by other things that are out of alignment.

At this point, I had closed my e-commerce business and I was not considering starting or joining any new startups. I had worked in a social enterprise that was a great fit, but I learned my talents and passions were less in business-to-consumer and more in business-to-business environments. I had been a nomad for enough years to want to settle down for a while back home with my dog. I had enough years morphing my lifestyle from a Jimmy-Choo-rocking attorney to a flip-flop or even barefoot nobody dancing through life, and I knew what the bare minimum Money circle needed to be for me to survive and be reasonably happy.

That's when the universe got the message I had sufficient clarity in what I was looking for and maybe I was ready for a star alignment moment. I went to a little sharing session by a vegan advocate who was running a nonprofit and working a full-time job as a designer for an online vegan business. After the session, I introduced myself and asked the speaker, "How can I be like you? I want to dedicate my vocational life to helping animals. These are my credentials, and I want to find a position where I can most effectively contribute my skills and experience to create the biggest impact." It was a long time building up to me being able to articulate this question as clearly as I did.

She said, "I know of three job openings." One was consumer-facing and advocacy-based—out; the other required me to move to Berlin and know German—out; the third was this one: Good Food Institute (GFI), a nonprofit working on shifting the world away from industrial animal agriculture.

Its theory of change was refreshing. Instead of advocacy or "consumer education," it was harnessing the power of innovation and markets to create paradigm shift to support the creation of alternatives rendering conventional products and methods obsolete. When smartphones came about, there was little "advocacy" required to convince people to move on from their Nokias; digital photography took over film; automobiles replaced horse-drawn carriages. The same thing could happen to industrial animal agriculture when better methods of production create products that outperform the conventional meat, egg, and dairy products.

When I joined GFI, it was in its third year. Having grown from three to about forty people, it was starting to expand globally. There were two international managing directors already on board creating GFI's strategies and establishing its operations in Brazil and India, respectively. The next managing director they were looking for was to build up the industry in China and East Asia. That's where I came in.

By now, you know my résumé and experience better than most employers who hired me. You must have noticed it was a stretch for me to be the founding manager of an affiliate organization to a food industry nonprofit. I have proven myself to be an inadequate founder; I knew nothing about managing a nonprofit (or any type of company for that matter) and I had zero experience in the food industry. I was not who I would go for to break into a new market, let alone one as challenging as China.

I wasn't intimidated, though, because I had no idea how big the job would turn out to be.

## THE BIG, BIG JOB

I saw the four circles intersecting and I grasped the opportunity without thinking twice. I had been waiting for this moment for too long.

A week into the job, I realized I was Spider-Man. Correction: I was Peter Parker.

Let me back up a little. Sorry, comic fans, I only know enough to make a Marvel Cinematic Universe analogy of Iron Man and Spider-Man's father-son dynamic (Harn, 2020). Iron Man took on the teenage, new-at-having-superpowers Peter Parker like a protégé. Originally as a local city-crime-fighting hero in *Avengers: Infinity War*, Peter Parker fought at a higher level beyond the scope of this planet alongside non-humans such as Thor—who is literally a god (Marvel, 2021).

That was how I felt joining the GFI team. I was Peter Parker. I looked around me and there was Iron Man, Scarlet Witch, and even the Hulk. I was standing among a team of superheroes.

GFI's founder and executive director is most like Iron Man—or I should say, Tony Stark. Maybe not a playboy and billionaire, but definitely a genius and philanthropist. In fact, he is often like a boy, playful and eccentric. He'd run toward instead of away from danger. It takes a fearless leader to forge a new way of doing business (including nonprofit business).

Our director of corporate engagement was most like Scarlet Witch, said to be the most powerful among the Avengers. She brought with her thirty years of experience in business, from working on big accounts like Levi's and Taco Bell to building her successful business on affiliate marketing through the dot-com boom. "I loved the thrill of closing deals," she said. She closed her marketing agency of twenty years to join GFI. That's badass.

Then our director of science and technology was a cell and developmental biologist with the knowledge and experience in the life sciences industry to ensure that "creating paradigm shifts" was not just an empty claim. I saw with my own eyes the powerful shift he inspired in others, whether we were meeting with the CEO of a food production giant, renowned professors and researchers at the most prestigious institutions, influential investors, or policymakers. It was like witnessing Bruce Banner, the shy physicist, transforming into the big, green, Incredible Hulk.

We worked and grew like a startup. It was intense. In the two years after I joined, the staff size exceeded the 150 mark and we were operating in the US, Brazil, India, Israel, Europe, and my piece of the pie, the Asian Pacific. I kept witnessing how a North Star job could attract the most amazing talent. When we hired the managing director to found our Europe organization, the person who ended up taking on the role used to be special adviser to UK Prime Minister, David Cameron, and a MBE. Yes, a member of the Most Excellent Order of the British Empire, the third-highest ranking Order of the British Empire award behind CBE and OBE. I was calling him my peer. That was insane.

This ensemble of extraordinary people came together to work toward one aligned mission. A shared North Star was the key. I could not imagine assembling people of that caliber and having them fall right into place as if they had been working together for years without that magical glue. I was mortified, but at the same time immensely proud to be part of the Avengers.

The things we achieved together blew my mind. I've never had a job where reading our organization's monthly reports would bring happy tears to my eyes.

Here are examples of what I typically experienced in our "ordinary course of business": Our Brazil MD convinced a big food producer to divert the funding that would have otherwise gone into building a new egg-producing facility to be invested in launching its first plant-based meat product line; our Sustainable Seafood Initiative and Startup Manual got honorable mentions in Fast Company's World Changing Ideas 2019 award; we partnered with the Indian government to establish a Centre of Excellence in Cellular Agriculture for cultivated meat research to grow real meat directly from animal cells without breeding and killing an animal (Clendaniel, 2019).

GFI's programs played a significant role that led to a 1,200 percent increase in the number of companies and organizations working in the alternative proteins industry within only three years. According to GFI research, the three pillars of alternative proteins received $4.4 billion in investments in the ten years from 2010 to 2020. Almost half, or $2.1 billion, was raised in 2020 alone. Cultivated meat companies received more than $360 million in investments in 2020, which is 72 percent of the amount raised in the industry's history (an industry only started in 2016). Fermentation companies devoted to alternative proteins have raised more than $1 billion in investments since 2013, 57 percent of which was raised in 2020 alone (Keerie, 2021).

I had my share of breakthroughs too.

Just like we can't bet on everybody doing the right thing for the greater good to change the world, no matter how advanced plant-based meat biomimicry techniques may become, some people will continue to only want the "real thing." Therefore, at least part of the solution to the dilemma of balancing consumer demand and harm to the environment and animals ought to be in revolutionizing the production method of animal meat.

I saw hope of a tipping point when cellular agriculture advanced to a stage such that commercialization was foreseeable. It has become a possibility to grow real meat from a small sample of animal cells without the need to kill animals. This product is cultivated meat. Instead of raising a live animal as the production unit of the end product of meat, the production unit can be a non-sentient bioreactor instead. This means taking the inevitable negative impact to environment and animal welfare (including human—think of slaughterhouse workers) as well as depletion of natural resources associated with animal agriculture out of the equation. The huge potential presented by cultivated meat was also what convinced "Scarlet Witch" to close her business and join GFI to create paradigm-shifting changes in the world.

We started promoting cultivated meat research to the government of Singapore in 2018 as a novel food production method. They came to our industry conferences. We arranged site visits, facilitated private meetings with cultivated meat startups, and continued to support research and analysis we share freely with our stakeholders. We were supporting the handful of cultivated meat startups around the world at the time. That number has grown a lot since. I still remember when the first cultivated seafood company from Singapore had its first press conference to showcase its prototype product, a cell-cultured shrimp dim sum, and I was invited as one of three tasters. The next day, I got a message from my Singaporean ex-colleagues back in my days in the financial world.

"Elaine, you're on the front-page news here!" The message read. I was barely awake and thought, *Oh no, what have I done this time?*

I had all bets on Singapore scoring the world's first regulatory approval for the sale of cultivated meat but still couldn't dare believe it when it happened.

In December 2020, a dream-come-true series of events occured. We were looped in by the food regulator and the company involved to assist with the announcement of the world's first-ever cultivated meat product to go on the market in Singapore. Shortly after, our Israel team held a press conference where the Israeli prime minister, Benjamin Netanyahu, became the first head of government to taste cultivated meat on camera—a landmark moment in the global race to bring cultivated meat to market (CISION, 2020). By

January 2021, my staff in Singapore was already eating dishes cooked with cultivated meat in a restaurant.

All of this happened within three years.

That experience will forever give me confidence that we can indeed change the world.

It is possible.

## CREATING NORTH STAR JOBS

It's only in hindsighI realized we were changing the world in another significant way: the creation of jobs allowing people to have the magical intersection of Talent, Market, Passion, and Mission.

As the person who accidentally found herself in a management position—fine, it was in the job title, which I subconsciously overlooked—my main responsibility was to build a sustainable structure that would grow and thrive so more and more people could make a living as well as an impact within that structure.

I must admit being a founder and manager is not within my genius zone nor am I "genetically coded" for being the person to hold space for everyone else to thrive. But if you are a born founder or professional CEO, imagine if you can build a company like this that would create many meaningful job opportunities for people who are looking for "second chances." This could really change the trajectory of their lives and the trajectory of our world.

An example is Renee Bell. She joined GFI in 2018 as editor and assistant for the science and technology department. Renee's background is in biology. When she had her fuck-it moment to quit her career, she'd been with the same pharmaceutical company for a decade as a sales representative, selling what was at the time the most prescribed insulin in the world. Pharmaceutical sales is a lucrative job with a lot of fringe benefits. "They paid for 80 percent of my MBA; my car and insurance were paid, I never paid for gas, and my salary was great and came with quarterly bonuses."

But then in 2010 during a class for her MBA, her professor showed the documentary *Food Inc.* The film examines the industrial production of meat and concludes it is inhumane and unsustainable—not only environmentally but also economically. It investigates the economic and legal power of major food companies that perpetuate a broken system based on profiting from supplying cheap but contaminated food. "I walked out of that room like, 'I'd never be eating meat again,'" Renee recalled. "It was one of those pivotal moments in life that changed the course of things."

Renee, in her personal life, turned vegetarian and then vegan; she started learning about the implications of eating a plant-based diet. In her work life, she continued to sell the insulin, but knew that with lifestyle changes, Type 2 diabetics can manage their disease instead of necessarily needing insulin. With this new knowledge about how insulin should really be down the line of the treatment options and how plant-based diets could help people manage their disease effectively, a huge cognitive dissonance started to develop in Renee's world.

"Here I was, day to day, going to physicians and saying, 'You should get your patients on this drug sooner because it will help manage their disease and keep their diabetes under control,'" said Renee. "My goal at work is one thing, but in my personal life, I'm learning all of these other things that completely conflict with what I'm doing at work." Renee finally quit her job and that industry altogether in 2016.

Now in her late forties with a husband in his mid-fifties who has spent his whole career in the electronic sales industry, Renee is trying to empower her husband to make the shift to purpose-driven work too. "We're getting closer toward the end of our careers, and it's so nice to have work that has meaning attached to it." Renee was recently promoted to science content specialist at GFI, and just before publication of this book, Renee told me with much excitement that her husband had also just handed in his resignation. He accepted an offer to join a healthcare nonprofit.

## TRANSFORMING THE JOB MARKET

It takes more than a few organizations to make it happen. In chapter one, we saw Christopher Michaelson's study with his business school students and their conclusion that they basically did not believe there was a job out there that would allow for the intersection of Talent, Market, Passion, and Mission (or that they would find their life purposes in their work). But with more and more organizations like GFI creating meaningful job positions, we may be able to change that.

One day, people may not even have to wait until their second careers to find purpose.

Another example is Nate Crosser.

"I wish I'd realized earlier just how powerful inertia is and how you know you'd end up in the average place if you just go into cruise control. The antidote to inertia is initiative, which is lacking a lot of the time," said Nate.

In the middle of our law degrees—fifteen years ago for me and five years ago for Nate—Nate and I actually interned at the same law firm: Dentons. It is now the world's largest law firm after a big merger. Nate admitted it was really hard to turn down a job offer to join Dentons because they "dazzle you with the majesty of the perks they can offer." But good on him for being so woke and realizing he felt soulless doing that kind of work. He "nipped it in the bud early." Yes, he meant his legal career. Nate's advice? Don't stick to the decisions you made when you were eighteen (which was when both Nate and I committed to law school). Something you signed up for at that age is unlikely to be what you do for the rest of your life. Nate took a year to figure that out while I took fifteen.

Nate became the innovation analyst at GFI, and what he created at GFI was beyond amazing. "We are the invisible hand of the alternative protein industry," said Nate. "We are the market builder."

Nate provided individualized startup support, from fund-raising strategy to go-to-market strategy consultations, built communities to connect industry players and facilitate collaborations, and evangelized the space through speaking at industry events. He's most famous for having co-authored open access resources, including the annual State of the

Industry Reports providing the basis of reliable data and insights encouraging immense growth of investment monies coming into the space, an increased number of startups and R&D initiatives, and every major food chain from Burger King to McDonald's to Starbucks to launch campaigns and incorporate plant-based items in their menus.

If you're reading this book and you're not mid-career, this is for you. Nate is twenty-six years old.

"It's so refreshing to be surrounded by people who were so mission aligned, and I realized that my number one thing when I look for business partnerships or to hire someone going forward, I'm just looking for the North Star alignment. If you have that, there will be very little friction because you're aligned with the shared goal," said Nate, as he embarked on a new venture to build his own company in the alternative protein space.

GFI put Nate in a highly leveraged position. In a very short amount of time, he became an expert in a newly created industry with only a handful of people who can call themselves experts. Nate's personal North Star is the mitigation of suffering, particularly animal suffering, and the mitigation of existential risk to life on Earth. And he will go out there and start a company with the same North Star as GFI to create alternatives to animal agriculture that improve outcomes for people, animals, and the planet.

One of the biggest impacts we may have created, albeit inadvertently, is the talent we train and feed back into the business world. Organizations like GFI are training grounds creating super effective and capable people with a strong sense of purpose and mission who will then go on to change the status quo in a big way.

This is exactly what Yvon Chouinard, the founder of Patagonia, preaches. Environmental stewardship is a main tenet of Patagonia's mission statement, and Chouinard takes it so seriously that he would go as far as assisting the competition to further his company's mission. As interest in corporate sustainability has grown, other companies have increasingly sought out Patagonia for advice. "I get calls from CEOs probably several times a month," said Chouinard. "We're very transparent about our journey" (Gunther, 2016).

A rising tide lifts all boats. This bigger mission to lift all boats in environmental sustainability manifested in some odd relationships like the one between Patagonia and Walmart, as well as the grand initiative called the Sustainable Apparel Coalition that consists of about 175 retailers, manufacturers, suppliers, and nongovernmental organizations. The coalition has built the Higg Index, a standardized supply chain measurement tool that creates a common language for companies to improve their environmental performance. With this bigger mission as the focus, Chouinard wants employees to learn everything they can about sustainability while working at Patagonia and then go into other companies and ignite changes in them too.

It is a circle of life. With Nate leaving GFI to create his own alternative protein startup, a vacancy was available for someone else to take on a North Star job—in came Sharyn Murray. Sharyn has spent the last decade of her career in one of the world's largest independent investment advisory and management firms where she had risen to be a top performing hedge fund research analyst. This year, she joined GFI as an investor engagement specialist responsible for crafting and executing a strategy to increase investment in the alternative protein industry.

Sharyn said, "As a subscriber to Effective Altruism, I had internally debated for years on the merits of continuing to 'earn to give' versus shifting to an Effective Altruism-oriented career. But after seeing the devastating impacts of the global pandemic, I decided it was time for a change."

Sharyn has worked within the investment industry for ten years at a large firm with access to a lot of people. She got to talk to CIOs and CEOs of hedge funds, senior executives at banks, pension and sovereign wealth funds, family offices, and foundations. "I think in the for-profit world, it was perhaps easier to get access to those relationships, and then I can bring those over because now a lot of them are personal relationships, and I think people in the for-profit space want to do some good," said Sharyn. Now she is excited to devote her career to improving animal welfare and reducing the harmful effects of factory farming on the climate and on the most vulnerable populations among us.

Something said by Isabelle Decitre came to mind. We met her briefly in chapter two. She shifted from being a star executive in the luxury brand corporate world to starting a venture capital company with a focus on sustainable and disruptive food solutions in the Asia-Pacific region. She said to me, "Not one day of this journey has been easy. But now that I've seen and experienced this new path, there's no way I'd ever go back to where I came from."

This is not about just one job. This is about going into the second phase of life, which may consist of a series of different work positions and capacities because we all continue to evolve. And we evolve fast in the second phase of life.

Like Nate, after two and a half years, I moved on. Yes, I had the dream job. It's fair to say I achieved many things alongside a group of the most capable and kind people that truly contributed to changing the world for the better and bringing the most promising solutions to the most pressing problems of this world.

But on a personal level, I had the ultimate breakdown and breakthrough.

I want to prepare you for the worst—the deep fall that comes with the second phase of life. Let me fill you in on the plot twist.

# PART III

# TRANSCENDENCE

# CHAPTER 8

# FALLING DEEPER TO RISE ABOVE

———

*"Self-love isn't selfish."*

−UNKNOWN

I remember feeling a tightness in my chest, then I started to have difficulty breathing. I've had experiences of panic attacks before, but this was many times more intense. I dropped to my knees and started involuntarily howling in anguish. Tears poured out of my eyes, and I rolled on the floor, desperately trying to grab something or someone or any kind of sense that could ground me.

I was using all of my strength to break myself out of this body like my life depended on it. But at the same time, it was as if I was already out of my body. I had no control of it whatsoever.

I didn't have the time to be broken. I just didn't. I needed to be fixed right away. In less than four hours, I had to go on stage and speak in front of eighty investors about alternative proteins. It was not the time to break. I begged my body, "Please, please, can you not do this now?"

That afternoon in November 2019, I experienced the onset of a nervous breakdown. It prevented me from working for weeks. I had to cancel business trips. I was physically unable to get to the airport and drag my body onto a flight, let alone dive into back-to-back meetings and speak on stage.

I didn't have any control over whether I could breathe from one second to the next.

Twelve years ago, the universe gave me a wake-up call in the form of depression. I was called to search for my life's purpose; I was called to gather the courage to quit my first career that looked successful on the outside but made me feel empty on the inside; I was called to build a vocational life that is the intersection of the four circles of **Passion**, **Mission**, **Talent**, and **Market**—a junction not shown on any map, that many people don't believe exists at all.

In hindsight, that wake-up call was an initiation to get on a path less travelled.

The initiation was never just about a career change.

Twelve years later, the universe gave me a further push in the form of a breakdown—with breakdowns come breakthroughs.

## MOUNTAIN, NOT MOUNTAIN, STILL MOUNTAIN

Real life is not a fairytale. I'm not here to tell a story that ends happily ever after.

I'd rather wish you an ever-evolving experience of transformation and transcendence.

*"See mountains as mountains, and rivers as rivers;*

*See mountains are not mountains, and rivers are not rivers;*

*See mountains once again as mountains, and rivers once again as rivers."*

Zen Master Qingyuan Weixin wrote that before he had studied Zen for thirty years, he saw mountains as mountains and rivers as rivers; when he arrived at a more intimate knowledge of life, he came to the point where he saw that mountains are not mountains and rivers are not rivers (Watts, 1951).

In my first career, I was seeing mountains as mountains. I conformed to the norms, I built my identity, and I climbed the societal ladder.

But then I began to question—beyond the norm, beyond the obvious, beyond the certainty. I let go of what I knew, what I owned, and what I was known for.

In my search for a second career, I saw mountains are not mountains. As I sought to discover the world and what I could do in this world— as a lawyer, a hippie, a yogi, an entrepreneur for profit or not for profit—the adventure looked like an external one. But the most fascinating journey all along was the one within.

That second phase of seeing mountains not as mountains was about the delusion of the ego, security and ownerships, and achievements and successes on the material level.

As I gained more clarity on my second career path (or the second phase of life) I started to come full circle.

Ultimately, the paradox must be resolved; mountain, not mountain, still mountain. As the Zen master taught, these are the three stages toward enlightenment. To see mountains once again as mountains was about transcendence on the spiritual level.

At this stage, my lesson was to learn fear and anger, self-doubt and guilt, and then forgiveness and compassion—all of these at a completely different level than I've ever experienced in the first phase of life.

## RETURN TO THE SELF

When I first discovered what was missing in my work and life, it was the circle of Mission.

Remember Mission (what the world needs) is the only circle without the word "you" in it. The others, Passion (what you love), Talent (what you are great at), and Market (what you can get paid for), all center around the self.

While the first phase of life is all about building one's identity and security, the second phase of life toward self-actualization is not about self-interest.

Or so I thought.

You know me well by now. With my idealistic tendencies and reactive temperament, I always take things too far and push myself to climb too high and fall too deep; sometimes quite literally (I'm obviously still mad about that treetop challenge in Bali). There is a middle way between self-interest and being altruistic. The second phase of life is not about sacrificing ourselves for the bigger good. I had to learn that the hard way.

But I'm not the only one. That's why I need to tell you these cautionary tales.

I had heard more than a few hammered, burned out do-gooders ask this question: "I'm just trying to do some good, do the right thing. Why do I feel like I'm being punished for being good?"

This struggle can range from a lack of work-life balance to more serious adversities.

For many, it's the constant struggle with a lack of resources. It's particularly hard for those who could otherwise easily command a six-figure income by sticking with a "normal" job to find themselves scraping for money here and there just because they chose a different path for the greater good. These do-gooders are not trustee babies; they are single mums or have a family to support or are paying off student loans and mortgages.

For others, it may be the fallout with people they had built their vision and mission together with. For some, it's the continuous conflict with their families that don't understand their career choices and thire consequences, whether that's more financial stress, less time for the family, more uncertainty for the future, or all of these combined.

For many, it's the emotional fatigue and development of secondary traumatic stress through working with victims at the forefront witnessing the worst of pain and suffering in this world on a daily basis.

The truth is, if you are encountering these adversities during a conventional first career, you would have quit much sooner. If a job is not paying you, if it's corroding your relationship with your family, or if it's causing you PTSD, the logical thing would be to remove yourself from the position. That should be an easy enough decision in a conventional career where you are primarily seeking to make a living, but if you are in a second-phase-of-life type of career, doing what you do for a mission with a capital M, you may feel a lot more moral obligation to keep going and push through the hardship.

Everyone has their own story, and here is mine.

## LEARNING HUMILITY
I was born and bred in Hong Kong, which had been a British colony since 1842. My grandparents fled to Hong Kong from

China to escape the Cultural Revolution, and I grew up listening to the horror stories of their family members being tortured during the revolution. For decades, Hong Kong and mainland China were cut off by a closed border; in fact, my grandmother was separated from her siblings who had failed to flee China and only reunited with them after many years of being apart.

Hongkongers have inherited a deep-rooted conflict. An ancestral, cultural, and political entanglement. Many of us have lived most of our lives under a free-market capitalist system: one that turned Hong Kong from a fishing village into a global financial center within a century. We are East meets West—Chinese with a Westernized value system. Then, in 1997, Hong Kong was officially "handed over" back to the communist China to be governed under the principle of "one country, two systems" (Wong and Mak, 2019).

In the ten years leading up to 1997, which were my childhood and teenage years, most of my extended family migrated to other countries. Every year I would say goodbye to more than a few classmates whose families had decided to migrate to Canada, Australia, the UK, the US, and all around the world wherever Hongkongers could earn a second citizenship as insurance. We as a people looked very prosperous on the outside, but a profound fear lurked underneath.

We as a people also looked excellent on paper as the bridge between the West and China as it gradually opened its market to interact with the world economy. We have the working ethics and values that fit seamlessly with the Western systems, the deep cultural link with the mainland Chinese, and the language skills to communicate with and between both.

I looked great on paper to be tasked with bringing GFI's important work to Asia—in particular, China.

I took the dream job but soon enough found myself in a conundrum. Without being registered, it was illegal for foreign nonprofits to carry on any activities in mainland China (Parkin, 2019). In a similar way, churches not denominated by the government in China were also considered illegal, which drove many Christian churches wishing to maintain their own sects to go underground despite the risk of punishment. For many pastors, it was a choice between breaking the law or being compromised to the movement called the Sinicization of all religions in China (Hadano, 2019).

The rules and redlines of law enforcement in China were constantly in flux. The ramifications of crossing those lines? Imprisonment was one of the possibilities and might not have been the worst.

I recall meeting a nonprofit manager threading that fine and moving red line.

"Can you turn off your social messaging app?" she asked.

"It's not on anyway, but why?" I responded.

"It's not enough that you're not using the app right now. You have to go into settings and turn off the sound and video functions—just to be sure."

*Are you being serious now? Are you fucking kidding me?* I remember thinking. I wasn't sure how to interpret the demeanor she exerted. She was obviously anxious but why and of what? That chilling air of walking on eggshells and paranoia of constantly having to watch over my back—I couldn't live like that.

As if that was not enough to freak me out, in the meantime, my home Hong Kong was falling into an abyss. Since 1997, countless pro-democracy protests and initiatives in Hong Kong to support maintaining the autonomy promised under the "one country, two systems" model haven't yielded much. On June 17, 2019, two million people went out on the streets (BBC, 2019). But no amount of people protesting could bring forth negotiation, let alone reconciliation. For what felt like the longest year that would never end, protesters and civilians alike lived in a constant state of violence. Anyone could be in a residential area and have tear gas fired at them or get attacked and beaten on the streets, in train stations, and in shopping malls (Hui, 2019; Sala, 2019; Hui and Steger, 2019).

At the end, a new national security law was imposed on Hong Kong said to be designed to crush any further anti-Beijing movement (Hernández, 2020).

A few months after the law came into force, I ran into my friend's husband at a bus stop. He was a dissident legislative council member.

"I'm going to jail tomorrow," he said. He was prosecuted under the new national security law.

I was too shocked to respond. The air between us seemed frozen, and time seemed to stop for a while until I was finally able to utter the words, "May I hug you?"

We hugged. That was all that I could do.

It was a moment of utter powerlessness and humility. I had never experienced anything like that in my life.

Or maybe that moment captured the essence of those few years I spent in constant distress and trepidation.

Outside of China, I was making headway in countries like Singapore. My team's work was truly changing the world. But regarding China—every effective altruist's dream where the most impact could supposedly be made—I was paralyzed by fear.

To do or not to do. The conflict within me was tearing me apart every day. If I had gone for it, it would have been like building a structure on quicksand. I would inevitably have to bring others into the quicksand with me. That was worse than fearing for myself. To feel fully responsible if anything were to happen to others, that was a whole different level of fear. On the other hand, if I had chosen to retreat, I'd blame myself for failing the mission.

I might have looked great on paper to execute the important work, but in reality, I sucked.

How much should I or anyone endure for this mission? How much well-being should anyone compromise for this mission? I didn't have any good or right answer except that over time, I was pushed to find out what was the answer for *me*. It was not about right or wrong, good or bad; simply an answer I was able to live with, that's all.

## PRESERVATION AND SERENITY

For a long time, I blamed myself. For a mission they believe in, some people endure living their lives with their personal safety and freedom threatened on a daily basis, from being bugged to being imprisoned.

I'm still seeking to resolve that profound guilt within me and accept I have limitations. My capacity is finite. My risk appetite is low. I need to forgive myself, or, as others keep trying to tell me, there is nothing to be forgiven. I seriously need to stop doing this to myself.

Not everyone is made for fighting on the front line. I can contribute in other ways.

"I've seen this many times before: people coming in with a big dream, willing to give everything they have to change the world. Unfortunately, these are the people who usually don't last in this field of work unless they change their perspectives." This comes from a friend of mine who's been in humanitarian aid for more than a decade.

Let's call him George.

I had a lot of preconceptions about his work. Originally, I was trying to get inspired by his bravery and endurance against adverse circumstances. George's work has taken him to countries including the Democratic Republic of the Congo and Afghanistan. While I might have surrounded myself with challenging geopolitical circumstances, George has literally positioned himself in war zones.

One of the things George did was manage projects making education available to children in remote villages where the government could not support them. He said in a passing-comment fashion, "That area was controlled by the Taliban. We needed a plan that allowed our staff to continue supporting the students and teachers in a way that was safe."

For me, that is terrifying. That proximity to danger—and not being born into it but choosing to put yourself in that situation in order to do work meaningful to you—is insane. It's beyond what I could ever deal with. To that, George would again in passing-comment fashion say, "Actually, as aid workers, we are very isolated and protected. It's not that bad."

Unlike me, George was not living in fear. Fighting fear and braving it on a daily basis would have paralyzed anyone and rendered them ineffective in their work. That is not the way.

George made it very clear that sacrifice and heroism has no place in the sustainable pursuit of mission-focused work. George was not sacrificing or compromising himself for the bigger mission. He was living with calculated risks he was genuinely capable of stomaching.

On top of that, George is gay, and his sexuality is not socially, or even legally, accepted in many of the countries he worked in.

He could have lived his life in other places where he could have held hands with another man in public and gotten married and started a family; instead, his work meant he had to live among incredibly conservative communities.

Was that, then, a sacrifice? Putting myself in his shoes, I can imagine that kind of inner conflict tearing me apart.

"I was twenty-three when I started in humanitarian work in Africa, and I was only starting to come out at that time. It was not a very important part of my life," George said. "At that time, my work was much more important to me."

What motivated George to go into humanitarian aid was to understand people who seemed to live in realities so far from his. In the beginning, he went in with curiosity and recognition that he was being welcomed into these communities as a guest. At that point in his life, he felt it was an acceptable balance—to be able to live among cultures that amazed him and do the humanitarian work that fulfilled him—while not being able to live entirely openly as a gay man.

"These are things that require generations and decades and centuries of change," said George.

Yes, changes take time. Changes take decades, if not centuries; war, severe poverty, disease, suffering, climate change, social injustice, and more. We are working toward progress;

we are planting seeds for the future. But in all honesty, most of us will not live to see the day of the final win. Nonetheless, we keep doing what we believe is right because it takes many, many steps to build that long staircase toward the light. Every step may look tiny in the grand scheme of things, but every step is needed.

This is a marathon, not a sprint.

What I ended up learning from George was not how to brave it but how to sustain. While I've had *reactiveness* and *distress* take over my work and life, George had *skillfulness* and *serenity* instead.

"There are moments in history for revolution, and there are moments for gradual change. And I think you just have to recognize that not every single moment is a revolutionary moment," said George. "That's unfortunate. But that's just a fact. And recognizing how to play a part in making gradual change is very important instead of being consumed by frustration and deciding you might as well not do anything."

And so it is. In recognizing that self-love and preservation are the foundation of going for the long haul with any mission, I finally found some peace and reconciliation with myself.

Next, I had to learn to reconcile with the world.

## CHAPTER 9

# BEYOND RIGHT AND WRONG

———

*"God, grant me the serenity to accept the things I cannot change, courage to change the things I can, and wisdom to know the difference."*

—THE SERENITY PRAYER

When you think of activists, what is the first thing that comes to mind?

My guess is the stereotype of the *angry activist*.

"My government makes me angry. The police force makes me angry. Homophobia makes me angry," said Zhanar Sekerbayeva, an LGBTQ and women rights activist from Kazakhstan. She had been attacked, arrested, and charged because of her sexuality and activism (Sekerbayeva, 2019).

Can anyone blame her for being angry? "Luckily, anger is what motivates me," she added. "Anger is my sister."

It's hard not to be angry as a changemaker, an activist, or an entrepreneur. And to me, these are all really the same thing—someone with a mission to challenge the status quo and shift the world from point A to point B.

Many of us moved into the second phase of life and shifted into second careers to do the *right* thing, to fight for the *right* cause, and to bring solutions to *right* what we believe to be problems. That can easily make us very angry at what we see as the *wrong* and the opposing forces.

The moment you decide to stop running from the world's problems and get up close and personal and even try to fix them, it's daunting. It's daunting to understand how big and complex these issues are and how relatively small and negligible our efforts may be. If you've chosen this path, you're certainly not enjoying the bliss of ignorance.

Looking at the darkness of this world in its eyes initiated me into this adventure. Indeed, that darkness is so deep and profound it dragged me into facing my darkest demons.

I have always had a reactive temperament. I could not stand to see injustice, unfairness, bullying, corruption, or good old-fashioned cheating and lying. I have a black and white world view. I'm Bomb in Angry Birds—the character that actually explodes when he gets too angry (*Angry Birds*, 2021).

Toward the second phase of life, instead of taking comfort in the fact that I'm at least contributing toward meaningful solutions to the world's problems, I became more and more angry—so much so that I scared myself more than a few times. Around my nervous breakdown, I went through each day feeling my blood was literally boiling in my veins and feeling a profound rage burning inside me.

I felt like Bomb, unable to control whether I would blow up from one moment to the next.

I had a rage problem.

Anger was not my motivation; anger was not my sister. I had to find someone doing good work but not consumed by anger and sweep my raging body with a fire extinguisher.

## THE DEEP DARKNESS

Pamela and I used to move in the same work and social circles. And that was such a small, protected bubble from the real world. We were both trained in one of the pedigree law firms and ended up specializing in finance law. Whenever people find me crazy and/or inspiring for how I've developed my career path, I say, "Look at Pamela." *That's* dramatic. What I did was nothing compared to her big leap.

More than ten years ago, Pamela's fuck-it moment happened at an unexpected end of a workweek when she was scanning the internet for sex trafficking news before leaving the office. That had become her new routine ever since her first church mission trip to Southeast Asia: learning about the human trafficking issues there.

But this time, a news story caught her attention.

US law enforcement had arrested three men outside of the US border and taken them back to the United States to be put on trial. The arrest was made under a US federal law with extraterritorial effect in cases of child abuse committed by Americans overseas. The article went on to describe the details of what these three men had allegedly done.

She read this in the news, packed her bags, and the rest was history. One of the arrested men had bought a thirteen-year-old boy from his mother for 2.5 US dollars and a bag of rice.

Overshadowed with a lot of self-doubt around "How can a twenty-something finance lawyer possibly be useful in fighting human trafficking?" but also armed with much faith that this was what God had prepared her for, Pamela left her job and moved to Southeast Asia. Soon enough, the path emerged. There was a big spectrum of things that needed to be done from rescue to rehabilitation, but where Pamela found herself fitting in perfectly was the job of setting up a nonprofit's legal department to support human trafficking victims through law enforcement and their legal proceedings. A lot of social workers and counselors had had to accompany these victims, mostly women and children, to court to testify against their perpetrators. Being a witness in a court case can be very stressful for anyone, let alone uneducated, trauma-tized, and exploited women and children who didn't have any grasp of their rights for availing the truth and bringing their perpetrators to justice.

So that's what Pamela did. She helped these women and children know their rights and learn to keep themselves safe. She conducted research and put in place mechanisms to improve the trial experience within the legal system that could often cause additional trauma for the victims. Of course, much of the problem was also with the thoroughly corrupt court system.

"The police, prosecutors, defense lawyers, even the judges, and basically everybody in the court have actually been bribed," said Pamela. "It was very common for foreign pedophiles to pay their way out of jail."

One experience stood out in particular.

"We had finally come to the trial," Pamela recalled. A wealthy American pediatrician who had spent about 150,000 US dollars to bribe everyone within the system and successfully delay the legal proceedings time and time again was finally at trial. Pamela was in the court with the three boys he had sexually abused.

When the much-anticipated court session finally started, the clerk suddenly announced it was going to be a closed court. Pamela's heart dropped. Without the public and media scrutiny, it meant anything could happen in that courtroom. The accused could get away without justice. Deep down, Pamela knew this was exactly what had been paid for under the table.

As she fought back tears while being pushed out of the court, Pamela was consumed with anger.

Everything reminded her of the story of the boy who had inspired her to drop everything and start a new career and life dedicated to helping these children. She was hit with the absurdity and cruelness of reality—a sex offender only had to pay a thirteen-year-old boy's mother 2.5 US dollars and a bag of rice to repeatedly rape him and 150,000 dollars in bribes to corrupted people within the system to evade an offender's responsibility for his crimes.

When Pamela was outside of that courtroom filled with anger, her husband challenged her to look at it from another perspective: the accused man was also broken by his sexual addiction, or maybe he was sexually abused as a child; every one of us at some point in our lives has made evil choices; God loves every single person, whether they are a murderer or a trafficker.

Her husband also consoled her with those wise words that I'm sure all of us have heard many times: the only person who would have been crippled by, and suffer from, that anger is the person who's angry, not the person inflicting the harm.

## ANGER MANAGEMENT

Pamela should have been angry, furious, and consumed with rage. Could anyone blame her if she was? But she turned that around and went back to her unshaken faith of doing God's work.

I struggled to understand.

I get it, but not really.

It's a similar kind of gracefulness I've seen in George. It's almost triggering for me.

Because why the hell are you not angrier? What's wrong with *you*?

Here's the thing with this second career path: even if I could get over being angry with myself because I'm no longer just sitting there doing nothing about what's wrong in the world, maybe I've gotten angrier with everybody else and the world instead.

While do-gooders find more compassion for others, it doesn't mean the world rewards them with more compassion or even bothers to give them a break and make their lives easier. It doesn't mean others in the world, or enough of them, are doing more good to move the needle together; in fact, oftentimes they'll find others in the world are doing the opposite of what good they are trying to create.

How are you not angry with the people taking bribes and denying the victims a fair trial, Pamela?

When your colleagues were being tracked and followed, when you and your kids might have been endangered because of retaliation from those trying to stop you from fighting the perpetrators and the system, how are you not angry, Pamela?

To protect you and your family, I can't use your real name in this book because anti-trafficking work is controversial in the eyes of the authorities. How are you not angry, Pamela?

I'm lashing out at Pamela because I've faced a lot less than she has while I've been consumed with a lot more anger. She works day in and day out, face-to-face with the epitome of evil, but she doesn't hate the world.

"My faith has everything to do with how I live my life," said Pamela. "Without knowing that God is in control of every-thing that happens in the world—the good and the bad—I would have felt very paralyzed in my own journey, grappling with this difficult question of why pain like trafficking exists in this world."

## LEARNING NON-DUALITY

I'm not religious, but I have followed enough spiritual teach-ers to know one of the keys of enlightenment is to move past the illusion of duality: the illusion of separateness and supremacy which is the root of many sufferings, from racism to sexism to speciesism. We tend to believe we are separate and another race or gender or sexuality or class or species or belief system (the list goes on and on) is somehow *less than* and therefore, a different or lesser or even cruel treatment of them is justifiable.

While I was still holding onto righteousness, holding onto duality, thinking that others opposing what I believed to be righteous were my enemies, was I any different from the acts and the people I believed were in the *wrong*?

For any changemaker, activist, or entrepreneur, with challenging the status quo being our core drive and what we do day in and day out, how do we not see the world in terms of opposites? *Good* versus *bad, right* versus *wrong, just* versus *unjust, positive* versus *negative*?

Does that inevitably mean *me* versus *you*?

Thousands of years ago, the poet Rumi wrote:

"Out beyond ideas of wrongdoing and rightdoing, there is a field. I will meet you there."

Where is that field?

Over time, I learned acceptance. I learned from spiritual teachers and healers; I learned from more graceful changemakers like Pamela and George that acceptance doesn't mean sitting there doing nothing. Acceptance is accepting the *conventional reality* for what it is. Yes, evil and wrong are happening right in front of us; but we seek to take the emotional charge out of our perception. Acceptance is being able to live with that conventional reality because it will take a lot of time and patience to create changes in that reality. In the long process of working to change that reality, we need to be able to live with the only reality we can perceive.

We need to have some peace. We need to reconcile within and without to be effective as changemakers.

Negative emotions and reactions put pressure on us physically. Our muscles tense up, our postures close up, and we have less space in our body. Not only that, we also have less space in our heads and our hearts. We are driven into tunnel vision, our thinking becomes even more polarized, our hearts close, and we become more intolerant of others; we fail to see those out-of-the-box solutions and possibilities.

For people who have faith, there is another *absolute reality*. Call it heaven, call it nirvana—that is the field Rumi talked about. The ultimate truth of interconnectedness and pure love may not be in the *conventional reality* humans are able to perceive with our very limited capacities, but they are in another *absolute reality* somewhere out there. If you believe we are spiritual beings having a human experience, we will one day meet again in that field beyond the right and wrong.

## HOW TO TRANSFORM SEPARATENESS

For now, this is all I have: some level of knowledge in my head and some level of true knowing in my heart that the true direction is toward connectedness within myself, others, and the world—not separateness. I can only trust I will continue to grow and evolve to one day truly live that wisdom.

In the meantime, there are always others around me I can learn from.

One of the most dramatic spectacles of separateness and of right versus wrong must be in a courtroom—and a courtroom of a murder trial, no less.

"The courtroom of a murder trial is almost like a wedding. All of the murderer's family sits on one side of the room. And all of the victim's family sits on the other side. It's a very, very, very strange thing to deal with," said Jennifer Stojkovic.

Jennifer was only twenty-two then, a year into new marital life with her twenty-three-year-old husband. Then her husband's best friend, the best man at their wedding, was murdered.

It's hard to imagine a more vivid image of duality than sitting in that courtroom.

"They're all sitting over there hoping he wins, and we're all sitting over here hoping he loses. It's very weird psychologically," said Jennifer. "In our particular case, there were like eight or nine videos of what had happened. The gun was passed around for the jury to see. So there's like a new trauma that emerges from a trial. We spent more than a year going through the grieving process, and then the trial reminded us of everything."

That was also the moment of choice. How do you even start to transform that kind of anger and destructive energy into something else, into anything but darkness?

Jennifer told me her story with a notably healthy amount of non-attachment.

Jennifer is the first and still the only person I know whose life was transformed so positively and magically by the murder of a loved one. I met Jennifer through being in the same circle of people building the post-animal bio-economy. She is the founder of the Vegan Women Summit, a relatively new endeavor of hers, born out of surviving the murder trauma and turning vegan.

I was almost a little lost. How were the two—surviving the murder trial and becoming a vegan entrepreneur—related? But then I found out, of course, that the link is compassion.

"Do we want to forgive this person, or do we want to stay angry and grieve forever? Do we want this person to hopefully learn from what he did, or do we want to lock him up and throw away the key and just be hateful and spiteful forever? My husband and I had a choice to make, and we both decided that we need to learn how to find compassion," said Jennifer.

That was the tipping point. Jennifer and her husband decided to forgive the person who had killed their friend. Her husband met the convicted murderer in prison and told him he had forgiven him. Jennifer has delayed PTSD from it; gun violence frightens her still. Her husband went through depression for about four or five years. But during it all, they found compassion.

"We realized that if we could find compassion for somebody who murdered our friend, how else could we find compassion in our life? And so the next obvious thing was, well, we're still eating animals. Three times a day, I was inflicting pain and suffering on another creature. If I want to be this compassionate person that I had decided to become, how could I leave that out? And so it immediately made sense for us to go vegan."

Compassion transforms fear into love and anger into freedom. I've been consumed by fear and anger these past years, but Jennifer's story is a much more personal experience of fear and anger. She could have let that fire of fear and anger define her life, but instead she chose forgiveness, and that fire was purified into a fuel of rebirth and creation.

With her privileged position of being a lobbyist representing technology companies like Google, Salesforce, Microsoft, Airbnb, and Twitter, Jennifer took her career assets to create the new venture that is the Vegan Women Summit.

Seeing food technology as the next big technology that could change the world for the better, Jennifer wants to make it happen. Jennifer is now leveraging her network and experience in the Silicon Valley community; through founding the Vegan Women Summit as a platform, she fuels the future of food through female leadership.

"I want to take everything I've learned from the tech industry to accelerate food tech; and I want to accelerate it in a way that includes women and people of color because the tech industry treats women and founders of color like shit, and we can do better."

In moments of immense tragedy or adversity, we can find a way to peel back those layers of intense pain and despair to crack our hearts open and let in the light. Anger is our defense mechanism against powerlessness, and powerlessness is what slowly but surely eats up our soul.

"The best thing you can do is find something to give you purpose; I call it a North Star. Find something that drives you in those really, really difficult days when it just all feels really helpless. Have something bigger than yourself. And even on the worst days, know that you've got something worth fighting for," said Jennifer.

The worst thing that has ever happened to Jennifer was also the best thing and made her the person she is today.

## CHAPTER 10

# THE ALCHEMY

———

*"The answer to an impossible situation*
*is to find the impossible solution."*

–PAUL WATSON

I'm calling this last chapter The Alchemy because one, if you are still reading this, you shouldn't be startled that I'm throwing something mystical and metaphysical at you again; and two, developing a fundamentally altruistic and purpose-driven vocational life is indeed an alchemical pursuit.

Alchemy is the process of purification and transformation. The quest is sometimes referred to as the Great Work and is symbolized by a three-stage process. I honestly did not know this when I first started writing this book in the three parts of dissolution, evolution, and transcendence.

The similarity between the process of alchemy and the journey of career change actually startled me.

Alchemy was always as much about a spiritual transformation of the soul as it was about a chemical change from lead to gold. It has even been suggested that chemistry is merely a disguise of what alchemy really was: an alternative spiritual pursuit that would otherwise have been oppressed by the medieval church at the time. Real alchemy was as much an outer process as an inner one: the transformation of matter as well as the alchemist (Kingsnorth, 2018).

In a very similar way, I know that for me, this creation of a second career has been so much more than changing my job; it has been a work of the soul and a pursuit of the spiritual.

We should seek to become alchemists to "transmute base metal into gold, suffering into consciousness, disaster into enlightenment," like Eckhart Tolle wrote in *The Power of Now* (2004).

If we are all alchemists on this journey of vocational self-actualization, what is the purifying fire fueling us on this quest?

## THE POWER OF INTENTION

Through the breakdowns and breakthroughs, I've learned this much: anger and resentment, anguish and despair, and aversion and hostility are not sustainable fuels but chronic poison to the mission and the soul.

Maybe the focus shouldn't be on the problems, ultimately.

Solving problems is only what we see on the surface, but as Robert Fritz wrote in *Path of Least Resistance* (1989), there is no such thing as "creative problem solving." Problem solving can never be truly creative because one is already limited by the problem itself as a starting point. Creativity goes beyond the confines of thinking and acting at the same level or in the same frequency as the impossible problems.

Maybe that is how impossible solutions are created, ultimately.

Problems are not inspirational. They are hardly the birthplace of enjoyable and sustainable endeavors. Anything not enjoyable is also unlikely to be sustainable.

The true essence lies in our intention—the original, pure drive that initiated our action. It took me some time to realize this.

The starting point for George was his curiosity about the African continent. He took a job that uniquely positioned him to be among the African people and learn about their cultures. The nature of the job was humanitarian work, but that journey originated from love and admiration of the people and their culture. That's why he was able to dedicate himself to bringing education to those who otherwise would not have had the opportunity while being patient that his sexuality was not something these cultures embraced.

It was a culture and a people he had love and admiration for, nonetheless. That original intention saved him from being sucked into resentment and losing his focus on what he was there to achieve.

In the spirit of not relying on being powered by the problem itself, here is something interesting about what increases the acceptance of homosexuality. Countries with higher levels of education have been found to be significantly more likely to say homosexuality should be accepted in society. In Kenya, between 2002 and 2019, the acceptance of homosexuality jumped from 1 to 14 percent as education level in the country rose (Poushter and Kent, 2020). George's work in education may have yielded a more effective outcome to homosexuality acceptance by creating a favorable environment for its growth, rather than directly fighting for the cause.

In the case of Pamela, her original intention was simply her love for the children. What motivated her was not to fight the perpetrators or the system. "I'm so compelled for these individuals to know their worth and to see new hope in their lives. Everything else is kind of in the periphery. It's not what I focus on," she said.

Her purity of intention that lies in love saved Pamela from being sucked into what could have easily turned into hatred toward the corrupt system that perpetuates human trafficking.

## BACK TO THE FOUR CIRCLES

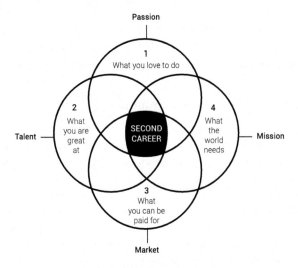

What was my intention?

I was depressed. I was looking for my life's purpose. I was angry with the state of the world and enraged by the exploitation of animals to support every aspect of human life. I had much contempt for the human species and speciesism—the suffering we cause to all animals, including ourselves and the planet we live in.

Did I mistake *passionately* hating something as *Passion*?

Now I know it probably doesn't count. Oops!

I hate what's wrong with the food system, but that doesn't mean I'd love working on what's gone wrong.

If you've been paying attention, you may be thinking, wait, did I just spend a few hours reading a book about someone who quit her first career, tried to build a purpose-driven second career, thought she landed a dream gig, then realized she had made a mistake, and she quit again in the end?

I want to say yes, just to see your face right now.

Well, I can guarantee you I will soon have another break-down (hopefully followed by a breakthrough) because that's just life. I'm choosing to finish telling this story on a relatively satisfactory note.

To bridge to my next move, I need to tell you more about Alison. She's the Scarlet Witch I mentioned in chapter seven. Scarlet Witch is the most powerful among the *Avengers*, and Alison is one of the coolest people I've met and worked with at GFI—or ever.

I've always thought Alison's job was one of the toughest among us. As the director of corporate engagement, Alison (being a vegan herself) mingled with big meat executives day in and day out. She recalled them being very cold to her at first, thinking she was the enemy, but she and her team successfully developed strong relationships with the biggest meat companies in the world in less than four years. The resulting impact to the mission was within that time, four of these mega meat producers have launched plant-based product lines, and two of them have invested in cultivated meat—producing meat from animal cells without raising and slaughtering a living animal (GFI, 2018).

If I had been in the same situation, I would have gone to either two extremes: thinking these executives were the enemy of our mission and failing to do the job because of my hostility toward them, or choosing to hide my true self and undermining my values in order to build rapport with them (which is unlikely to work in the long run).

That's not how Alison approached it. The foundation of her effectiveness is going into a boardroom and negotiating with humility. She tries to find the humanity in people; the common ground.

Because at the end of the day, we are all same-same. "I have broken bread with many of these executives, and several have revealed that their wife or daughter or son is vegetarian," said Alison. "And it's opened their eyes to other ways of thinking about food."

Alison's authentic drive is her love for food and nutrition, in addition to her love for animals.

"Food has always been such an important part of my life," Alison said with sparkles in her eyes. "Even to the point that when I go on vacation anywhere, one of my favorite things to do is to go into a local grocery store. I would just look at the shelves to seek out the best foods. It's just something I love. I'm always learning and reading about nutrition, always trying to share what I know about food and nutrition with my friends."

That's common ground. That passion creates common ground whether you are a herbivore or omnivore.

What do I check out whenever I go on vacation anywhere? I can guarantee you grocery stores and restaurants are not on my list. Find me at the fashion boutiques, shopping arcades, and lifestyle stores selling pretty things nobody ever really needs but add flair to your life.

There. My eyes just sparkled.

## THE NEXT INTERSECTION

Over these years of ups and downs, I have gained more clarity and accumulated the experiences to land my next North Star role after GFI.

Animals are a constant for the fulfilment of my **M**ission circle, but I've found something that feeds the fashionista in me and scores higher in my **P**assion circle. I'm continuing to build what has now emerged in the world as a whole new thing: the post-animal bio-economy. Instead of disrupting the food space, I'm now using the success formula I learned at GFI to accelerate another new industry.

We are calling it the "next-gen materials" industry, which innovates with materials science to create sustainable and high-performance alternatives to conventional animal-based materials like leather, fur, wool, down, silk, and exotic skins—materials heavily used in the fashion, automobile, and home goods industries. Those materials come from (and are essential components of) the animal agricultural industry that causes the biggest problems in the world, like climate change.

As the chief innovation officer of a new nonprofit startup, I'm tasked with supporting materials innovators and accelerating investment into advancing materials science breakthroughs and commercialization.

Passion, Mission, Talent, Market (P-M-T-M): all checked. It's a great fit for a self-proclaimed fashionista plus animal rights activist with entrepreneurial, finance law, corporate, as well as nonprofit experience. Yes, that's me.

## THE GREAT WORK AND THE THREE MOUNTAINS

That's my story (so far) and the stories of other purpose-driven do-gooders, superheroes, and lost-and-found careerists I met on the way of this less travelled path.

The alchemy process, also called the Great Work, may look like a chemical transformation on the outside, but the true magic comes from the inner transformation of the alchemist. The outcome for the alchemist can be self-realization, communion with divinity, and fulfillment of purpose (Beyer, 2018).

Everyone on this journey of shifting to a second-phase-of-life career is an alchemist.

I've seen many alchemists on this path doing the Great Work; the Great Work of a three-stage process of blackening, whitening, and reddening a raw matter to break down, then purify, and finally transform.

Just like when we are doing work that brings promising solutions to the world's most pressing problems, creating impossible solutions for impossible problems feels like turning lead to gold.

In dedicating ourselves to meaningful work, we are transforming within. We break down our leaden and inert first phase of life; we let go and purify to find our essence; we transcend.

The vessel of transformation is the work we do of bringing light to the darkness in the world through our second career, driven by something bigger than our ego; we hope to change the world through our work while inevitably, we ourselves are transformed and saved through the work we do.

It's alchemical. It's magical. Dare I say, it's been quite a divine experience.

In the beginning, I was lost, as many others I had met in that phase of life were; I was rolling in the deep end of the rabbit hole of finding purpose in my life. I'd climbed the societal ladder in the first phase, but now what? I looked successful on the outside but was empty inside. I wandered purposelessly, rendered powerless and stuck.

Then there came a point when I couldn't lie to myself any longer. I had to begin the second-phase-of-life journey.

From receiving the wake-up call to declaring the fuck-it moment, I gathered the courage to quit everything familiar and safe. I had to overcome a lot of fear: the fear of choosing a path less travelled, losing other people's approval, and failing societal expectations. I was terrified of not belonging, but losing myself would have been worse.

It will feel like a fall from glory, but you are actually falling upward.

You jump, I jump.

Turn off the autopilot mode and unfollow the norm. Find out who you really are. If a shopaholic like me can become a hippie, even just for a while, you can do it too. Actually, unfollow my way too; do it your own way. As long as you detox and let go of the many structures, habits, and conditionings holding you down, you will free yourself and get on this big new adventure.

It will be an adventure within and without.

As you venture into this new path, it will inevitably be an intense self-discovery journey. You will have to find your own voice and learn to listen to your intuition and inner truth. On your way, you will find your higher purpose through persistently pursuing it.

You will also rediscover the world and your relationship with the world and others at a deeper level. What if you finally know that sweet spot that fulfills your Passion, Mission, and Talent, but then the Market is not there? What if there's no such job in the world?

I've seen alchemy at work. It's magical, it's serendipitous, and it's a force of enchantment.

The stars will align. If you've travelled this far from living a lie to awakening and beginning a journey to seek the truth, from being on autopilot mode, running on a treadmill going nowhere to gaining awareness and finding the truth within yourself, you are starting to become a creator in life.

Yes, the stars will align when you are ready.

It's not going to be easy. You've seen curve balls thrown at me and others even after we find the intersection of the four circles. All I can say is it will be worth it.

Find strength in community. The population of Great Work-doers is growing. These like-minded changemakers are out there somewhere. They are still a bit of an exotic breed. I've had to collect them like Pokémon over the years, but these little cute monsters are out there (and not only in augmented realities)!

Just like Pokémon, Great Work-doers evolve fast. This alchemical pursuit cultivates inner wisdom and compassion; you will evolve. Underneath it all, this journey is a transformation fueled by the universal truth that is love.

We may finally see mountains as mountains again.

We are walking the path wise men and women before us have paved more than thousands of years ago. This is a journey of dissolution, evolution, and hopefully, eventually, transcendence.

*"See mountains as mountains, and rivers as rivers;*

*See mountains are not mountains, and rivers are not rivers;*

*See mountains once again as mountains, and rivers once again as rivers."*

—ZEN MASTER CHINGYUAN WEIXIN

Mountain, not mountain, still mountain: the three stages toward enlightenment.

Transformations are all different, but also same-same. The ultimate truth is always same-same.

And that can be the story of your next forty thousand hours—or however many hours there are in the rest of your working life.

One day, we will reconcile with the paradox. We will comprehend the oneness of things. We will transcend toward all-encompassing understanding and enlightenment. We will get there one day by being light and bringing light into the world.

It's a profound experience; to fall into an illuminating subsistence is to fall into love.

# ILLUMINATE

———

*"True darkness is not the absence of light, but
the conviction that light will never return."*

I hope to leave you with a message of...hope.

It feels weird that I'm the person delivering this message.
You've seen me struggle through finding hope. I'm not a
naturally optimistic person. Quite the opposite; I'm clini-
cally depressed.

Maybe that makes the message even more convincing coming from me.

Every time I come out of meditation, I have a fleeting moment
of experiencing nirvana. As Buddhist monk and animal
rights activist Tashi Nyima says, meditation is "resting in
the empty luminosity" (Zacharias, 2019).

Then the clusterfuck of reality inevitably strikes again.

How can I, how can we, be luminous beings when we constantly feel like we are covered in feces (also known as impossible problems)? How can I, how can we, even begin to attempt to illuminate the world with what we do in our vocational lives?

On this path, I'm constantly surrounded by superheroes. Their superpowers are the same; at the end of the day, it's compassion.

When I was crying my eyes out through the darkest times, Francis said to me, "It's much easier to find darkness; our job is to find the good, find the light despite the dark."

We briefly met Francis in chapter two where his fuck-it moment turned him from a corporate executive into the "father of social enterprise" in Hong Kong. Over more than a decade, Francis has incubated and built more than forty social ventures. Then in 2019, a perfect storm came upon our city: rogue political turmoil and an unprecedented pandemic.

Our home reeks of a rotten odor of powerlessness. The city is dead. Hope is dead.

Being deeply embedded in work with the most vulnerable communities in society, it's hard to imagine how this perfect storm has impacted his work, his team, and his life.

"It's like I've been building a sandcastle," said Francis, with much sadness in his eyes. "One big wave hit, and everything is gone."

As tears ran down my face, I realized it wasn't only sadness I saw in Francis's eyes but a profound gentleness that held a safe space for me to open my heart again.

"But the way out of fear and anger, Elaine, is hope and compassion," said Francis. "This is our opportunity to restart." I learned from Francis how compassion can turn powerlessness into hope.

Choose to create light where we can. In the presence of light, darkness disappears.


## LOVE IS LIGHT

Did I begin this journey with hatred instead of love?

Or maybe in the midst of everything, I got lost and forgot.

Twelve years ago, a ball of white fluff came into my life. That was the one truest love I've ever experienced.

Before that, I had never received truly unconditional love, and I had never given truly unconditional love—no expectations, no comparison, no judgment. How many of us have been able to truly love another person so purely and powerfully? Most of us, truly, are not capable of loving our children, our partners, our parents, or ourselves without *any* expectations, comparison, and judgment.

The ball of white fluff was a puppy named Bunnie and came into my life after I was diagnosed with depression. She taught me true love. Not because she loves me unconditionally, but because I love and accept all of her unconditionally. That's the most precious gift the universe has given to me—showing me I have the capacity to love in this way, enabling me to experience the purity and truth that indeed resides somewhere within me: the great love that's too often overshadowed by the way I choose to react to the clusterfucks in the world.

Bunnie opened my eyes to an all-embracing love but also made me aware of evils in the world and the pet trade industry. Bunnie opened my heart to a cross-species connection that also inspired me to turn vegetarian overnight. And, of course, that shift then inspired a complete transformation of my career path and initiated me into the second phase of life.

It was love that initiated me. It wasn't hate.

## NEXT PHASE IN LIFE

Francis is now working with his team on a ten-year impact journey called Odyssey and is calling on all stakeholders in society to collectively shape a new urban vision for a better Hong Kong by 2030. The vision is a big one: zero substandard housing, meaningful youth engagement, a wellness city model, farm-to-urban sustainable living, aging-friendly innovations, plant-based food technology, and community economy. Many projects have already been activated to restart, reimagine, and rebuild.

Over in Massachusetts, Alison is now business development director in plant proteins for the global eight-billion-dollar conglomerate Kerry Foods. Alison's North Star is still to make sure plant-based meat, dairy, and eggs can win on taste and price. In her current position, Alison can leverage the plant-based ingredients portfolio of a highly influential food industry giant with a thousand research and development scientists to help food manufacturers make excellent meatless products.

Christine celebrated her son's seventh birthday in their home in Switzerland. It feels like a lifetime ago, or just yesterday, when she was on stage with him when he was a few months old, breastfeeding him backstage at the very first launch of Thought For Food. Actually, Thought For Food and my old team at GFI are partnering in the Thought For Food 2021 Challenge to incubate solutions that will help increase the value, utilization, and diversity of use of regionally relevant crops for alternative proteins in Asia.

What happened to Karuna, you ask?

His face is 100 percent fine now. When he's not swimming with whale sharks, he's exploring beautiful ancient caves and cenotes. That lucky son of a—no, it has nothing to do with luck, actually. Karuna made a conscious choice and this is the life he's set out to create since our paths first crossed five years ago.

Originally from Chicago, Illinois, today Karuna is living in Tulum, the site of a pre-Columbian Mayan walled city, one of the last cities built and inhabited by the Maya, now in the

Mexican state of Quintana Roo (Lonely Planet, 2021). His office view is sometimes like what we used to have in Bali; but frankly, the Mexican beach overseeing the Caribbean Sea looks even more beautiful.

Karuna is now the CEO of WaterNow. He's dedicating over two decades of environmental engineering expertise toward a big vision: a world where everyone has access to clean water. Because to Karuna, clean water is a basic human right. As the world stands now, one in ten people are without basic access to clean water, and diarrheal disease kills one child every sixty seconds (Lifewater, 2021).

Over the past five years, Karuna and his team have completed 188 projects serving over 55,000 people in eleven countries including Egypt, Colombia, Brazil, Ghana, Kenya, and where we first met, Indonesia. WaterNow tries to bring solutions to underserved and indigenous communities. Its mantra is "water is a unifier" to merge technology such as rainwater catchment and filtration and purification systems harmoniously with cultures affected by local and global industrialization, climate change, and pollution.

In the middle of 120 acres of land in the pristine jungle, Karuna's dream project is popping up and standing above the top of a sea of beautiful trees. Much like Karuna himself, this tree house that is equal parts sacred and playful stretches up toward the sky in its organic, fluid form. It's as if Gaudi's Casa Milà in Barcelona and the Green School in Bali made love and had a child. The geometrically irregular, sinuous architecture flows like water, and the structure seems to have a life force in its own—bending, curling, stretching, and yes, breathing.

No surprise there that this dream project of Karuna's utilizes materials like bamboo, which Bali's Green School was also built from, to achieve substantial and near-permaculture structures.

This is the regenerative eco-community Karuna set his mind to building five years ago. Phase one is to sustainably develop five acres for bio-construction homes with abundant cenote water springs. Houses will be solar powered with bio-digesters and microbes for the sewer system, rainwater catchment, a recycling center, composting, and regenerative water filtration. There will be a retreat center and a community garden with seed banks to be self-sufficient. This will also be the basis of replication and will offer working models to other eco-villages, hotels, and establishments for a new way of living in harmony with nature.

## BE THE LIGHT

People say, "Be the change you want to see in the world."

After years of ups and downs in this second phase of life, I'd like to invite you to be the *light* you want to see in the world—a softer perseverance that draws its power from love and is grounded in deep compassion.

Almost ten years ago, Karuna was on a vision quest in the Andes. As the first light of the day came through, the sound of twittering, vibrating movement awoke Karuna's senses. As he opened his eyes, his gaze met with a golden and purple hummingbird hovering a few inches from his nose.

As Karuna closed his eyes again, he received this message from the mysterious hummingbird, dancing mid-air in the delicate mist of dawn:

*"Appreciate all creation, re-awaken joy day and night.*

*Walk in beauty, laugh, stay inspired, and never forget the magic of being alive.*

*Learn life essence of love from flowers and birds, which do more than just survive.*

*Have simple courage, help restore balance and health to your-self, thrive."*

Time was frozen like he was in a dream, and the whole forest burst into the most vibrant of colors. Feeling much love from this hummingbird, Karuna wasn't sure if it was the morning dew or tears running down his face. It washed away sorrow and gave him the strength to fly high and free.

The bird continued to tell Karuna:

*"Remember to fight in a good way so that no one gets hurt,*

*And to smile and cherish the beauty of this rainforest and body Earth."*

The hummingbird's tiny, colorful feathers glistened in the air.

Glowing in beauty and joy, it suspended into a beam of light. The hummingbird disappeared into an aura of mysticism.

Looking over the beautiful jungle from the top of the tree house he had built, Karuna thought back to that moment of encounter with magic.

A dog or a hummingbird, a baby or flesh-eating bacteria: same-same. Have you received the sign?

May your magical journey begin.

# ACKNOWLEDGMENTS

---

First and foremost, I'm deeply thankful for my loving mum and dad. So far, I've only told you one side of the story. They may not be thrilled that I've chosen a less-travelled path (mostly worried that it's a more uncertain and challenging way of life), but they are also the ones I can count on to back me up no matter what. I'm extremely blessed to have parents who dedicated their lives to diligently providing for our family. My parents may not have had the chance to live like dreamers or hippies, but they are idealists too (I got that from them). They taught me to have a high standard of integrity and righteousness. Bottom line, as Japanese author Haruki Murakami said, "Between a high, solid wall and an egg that breaks it, [they] will always stand on the side of the egg." That's what I love most about my parents. I'm also deeply grateful for my amazing little sister, Denise, who takes care of me like a big sister and has to endure my melodrama for her whole life.

On this path of vocational self-actualization, I've had the honor of working with and learning from the most amazing people. We've grown from colleagues and acquaintances to trusted friends and allies for life. Some of you are mentioned in the pages of this book; many more of you are in my heart. I try my best to pay forward your wisdom and kindness in everything I say and do. We all stand on the shoulders of giants. I cannot imagine how much harder it was for the pioneers and fighters who chose this path fifty, thirty, or even just ten years ago. Thanks to everyone who came before us and paved the way. Special thanks to everyone at Green Monday, the Good Food Institute, and the Material Innovation Initiative for giving me the opportunity to be part of something truly magical. May each of these important organizations continue to flourish and create paradigm shifts in the world.

I'm very grateful for my early readers, Ryan Huling, Jen Rhymer, Nicole Rawling, and Rachel Pickel who provided invaluable feedback and tremendous help to enhance this work. I'm especially grateful for my best friend, Jen, who's been my primary support system through this second-phase-of-life journey. I also want to express deep gratitude to Professor Eric Koester for building the Creator Institute and the amazing book creator program that made my dream of publishing this book come true. Thank you to the New Degree Press team, especially my editors, Laura Buckley and Chelsea Olivia, for helping me bring this book to life.

Finally, this whole experience has been so humbling. To realize I'm blessed with so many people's love and support, even from people I met through work ever so briefly and classmates I've not seen for over twenty years, it's hard to put into words. Thank you, thank you, thank you to all friends old and new that supported my book:

Aaron Pang
Abhinav Mehra
Agnes Wong
Albert Tseng
Alexander Chan
Alexander Pestalozzi
Alexandra Clark
Alison Rabschnuk
Alvin Wong
Andrew Wong
Anne Green
Anna Tai
Anna Tai
Anri Shiga
Aproop Ponnada
Benjamin L. Hallen
Bev Postma
Bianca Kwong
Blake Byrne
Brian Van Langenberg
Bruce Friedrich
Carol Wong
Carolyn Li
Carrie Chan
Carrie Chung
Catherine Chu
Cecilia Chan
Chan Ka Kin
Cherie Choi
Cherry Kam
Christine Gould
Christine Miller

Christine Tsang
Clare Siu
Claudia Tam
Coco Tse
Cody Wood
Cortney Busch
Courtney Ngai
Daisy Ma
Dalal Alghawas
Dan Altschuler Malek
David Bucca
David Welch
David Yeung
Dean Powell
Denise Siu
Derek Chow
Diana Cheng
Dominic Wong
Donna W. Wong
Elaine J. Cheung
Emileigh Thylin
Emily Byrd
Eric Chan
Eric Cheng
Eric Koester
Eva Yoe
Fanny Tse
Fei Tan
Felipe Arguijo
Felix Lai
Fengru Lin
Feng Wenxu

Fiona Young
Flora Ho
Florence Ho
Francis Tso
Gigi Pang
Graham Miao
Gustavo Ribeiro Guadagnini
Humphrey Lee
Ingrid Cheng
Irene Chan
Isabelle Decitre
Jackie Cheung
Jacqueline Kravette
Janice Hui
Jeffrey Chau
Jennifer Law
Jennifer Lamy
Jennifer Tsang
Jen Rhymer
Jenny Ng
Jonathan Liu
John Cheng
John Eng
Johnny Chan
Josh Balk
Karen Tam
Kate Po
Kathlyn Tan
Ka Yee Chan
Kristie Ho
Gillian Lam
Laura O' Connell

Liana Cheung
Lila Wong
Li Lian Khoo
Ling Ka Yi
Lupemaria Beal
Ma Chi Hong
Maisy Chan
Malisa Ng
Mary Tse
Michael Fong
Michal Klar
Michelle Tse
Mike McCormick
Minqi Wang
Mirte Gosker
Mitchell To
Monica Park
Naoto Yamaguchi
Nate Crosser
Nick Halla
Nicolas Stoeckert
Nicole Rawling
Nir Goldstein
Nydia Zhang
Pamela Leong
Park Benjamin
Peony Yung
Phoebe Yuen
Plato Wai
Po Chu Wai
Queenie Lau
Rachel Pickel

Regina Cheung
Rita Fong
Rose Convery
Rosie Wardle
Ryan Huling
Ryanne L.
Samantha Ogle
Samuel Yee
Sanah Baig
Sandhya Sriram
Sherry Wong
Simon Newstead
So Hiu Pan
Stephanie Downs
Suet Kei Kong
Susan Halteman
Sharyn Murray
Sydney Gladman
Tadd Hatcher
Tam On Yee
Tanja Wessels
Terry Ng
Thomas Knudsen

Toube Benedetto
Tse Quincy
Uzial Hsieh
Varun Deshpande
Victoria Law
Vincent Tam
Vikas Garg
Vivek Viswanathan
Vivian Fung
Vivian Loke
Will Schafer
William Siu
William Wong
Winefred Kwan
Winnie Li
Winnie Sham
Winnie So
Wong Chi Keung
Worm Engineer
Yiu Bosco
Yu Tse Heng
Zeng Wanyi
Zhi Qing Ho

# APPENDIX

---

## INTRODUCTION

Businesswire. "Workers Value Meaning at Work; New Research from BetterUp Shows Just How Much They're Willing to Pay for It." News. November 7, 2018. https://www.businesswire.com/news/home/20181107005201/en/Workers-Value-Meaning-at-Work-New-Research-From-BetterUp-Shows-Just-How-Much-They%E2%80%99re-Willing-to-Pay-for-It.

CB Insights. "Your Startup Has a 1.28% Chance of Becoming a Unicorn." Research Briefs. May 25, 2015. Accessed on June 27, 2021. https://www.cbinsights.com/research/unicorn-conversion-rate/.

O'Connell, Brian. "The Search for Meaning." SHRM. March 23, 2019. https://www.shrm.org/hr-today/news/all-things-work/pages/the-search-for-meaning.aspx.

Orr, David. *Ecological Literacy: Educating Our Children for a Sustainable World.* San Francisco: Sierra Club Books, 2005.

Rohr, Richard. *Falling Upward: A Spirituality for the Two Halves of Life.* San Francisco: Jossey-Bass, 2011.

Wade, Cleo. *Where to Begin: A Small Book About Your Power to Create Big Change in Our Crazy World.* New York: Atria Books, 2019.

Watts, Alan. *The Way of Zen.* New York: Pantheon Books, 1951.

## CHAPTER 1

Collins, Jim. *Good to Great: Why Some Companies Make the Leap and Others Don't.* New York: HarperCollins, 2001.

*DruckerInst.* "Jim Collins Drucker Day Keynote." May 13, 2010. Video, 59:48. https://www.youtube.com/watch?v=7qZP4kaY-cXU.

Frankl, Viktor E. *Man's Search for Meaning.* Boston: Beacon Press, 2006.

García, Héctor and Francesc Miralles. *Ikigai: The Japanese Secret to a Long and Happy Life.* New York: Penguin Books, 2017.

Michaelson, Christopher. "The Importance of Meaningful Work." *MIT Sloan Management Review*, January 1, 2010. https://sloan-review.mit.edu/article/the-importance-of-meaningful-work/.

Nakanishi, Noriyuki. "'Ikigai' in Older Japanese People." *Age and Ageing*, Volume 28, Issue 3, May 1, 1999, Pages 323–324. https://academic.oup.com/ageing/article/28/3/323/31016.

Rohr, Richard. *Falling Upward: A Spirituality for the Two Halves of Life*. San Francisco: Jossey-Bass, 2011.

Winn, Marc. "What Is Your Ikigai?" The View Inside Me. May 14, 2014. http://theviewinside.wpengine.com/what-is-your-ikigai/.


## CHAPTER 2

Allinder, Sara M. and Janet Fleischman. "The World's Largest HIV Epidemic in Crisis: HIV in South Africa." Center for Strategic & International Studies. April 2, 2019. https://www.csis.org/analysis/worlds-largest-hiv-epidemic-crisis-hiv-south-africa.

Association for Professionals in Infection Control and Epidemiology. "Get the Facts about Necrotizing Fasciitis: The Flesh-Eating Disease." Monthly Alert for Consumers. Accessed on June 27, 2021. https://apic.org/monthly_alerts/get-the-facts-about-necrotizing-fasciitis-the-flesh-eating-disease/.

Beyer, Catherine. "Peyote and the Native American Church." Learn Religions. August 27, 2020. https://www.learnreligions.com/peyote-and-the-native-american-church-95705.

Marson, Anthony G. and Salinas R. "Bell's palsy." *West J Med.* 2000 Oct. 173(4):266-8. https://www.ncbi.nlm.nih.gov/pmc/articles/PMC1071111/.


## CHAPTER 3

*ARASHI's Diary–Voyage–*. Limited Series, episode 16, "OHNO's Diary." Released 2019, on Netflix. https://www.netflix.com/hk-en/title/81219073.

Chan, Wing-tsit. *A Source Book in Chinese Philosophy*. Princeton: Princeton University Press, 1963.

Fuji Television Network. "VS ARASHI." Accessed on June 27, 2021. https://www.fujitv.com/variety/vs-arashi/.

García, Héctor and Francesc Miralles. *Ikigai: The Japanese Secret to a Long and Happy Life*. London: Penguin Life, 2017.

*GaryVee TV*. "Hasan Minhaj, Homecoming King, White House Correspondents Dinner & Immigrant Parents | AskGaryVee 274." December 4, 2017. Video, 1:28:40. https://www.youtube.com/watch?v=ypMm1-jhZ34.

*HYBE Labels*. "BTS (방탄소년단) 'Blood Sweat & Tears' Official MV." October 9, 2016. Video, 6:03. https://www.youtube.com/watch?v=hmE9f-TEutc.

Kyodo News. "Arashi Stepping Out of Celebrity Storm to Seek New Life." *The Jakarta Post*, January 29, 2019. https://www.thejakartapost.com/life/2019/01/28/arashi-stepping-out-of-celebrity-storm-to-seek-new-life.html.

IMDb. "Shô Sakurai." Accessed on June 27, 2021. https://www.imdb.com/name/nm1123941/.

McIntyre, Hugh. "8 Ways BTS Made History at The Billboard Music Awards." *Forbes*, May 25, 2021. https://www.forbes.com/sites/hughmcintyre/2021/05/25/8-ways-bts-made-history-at-the-billboard-music-awards/?sh=62d5900eb646.

Official Charts. "Adele." Accessed on June 27, 2021. https://www.officialcharts.com/artist/3710/adele/.

*Oricon News.* "嵐、最新シングルが自己最高初週売上で初登場1位に歴代1位の「通算1位獲得数」を54作に自己更新【オリコンランキング】(in Japanese)." *Oricon Music*, August 4, 2020. https://www.oricon.co.jp/news/2168568/full/.

Stock, Mark. "Arashi is the Most Popular Band You've (Probably) Never Heard Of." *The Manual*, August 6, 2020. https://www.themanual.com/culture/arashi-jpop-most-popular-band-in-world/.

Watanabe, Ken, Kazunari Ninomiya, Tsuyoshi Ihara, Iris Yamashita, and Paul Haggis. *Letters from Iwo Jima*. Burbank, CA: Warner Home Video, 2010. DVD video.

## CHAPTER 4

Rohr, Richard. *Falling Upward: A Spirituality for the Two Halves of Life*. San Francisco: Jossey-Bass, 2011.

Shames, Laurence. *Not Fade Away*. New York: Harper Perennial, 2004.

## CHAPTER 5

Eisenmann, Tom. "Entrepreneurship: A Working Definition." *Harvard Business Review*, January 10, 2013. https://hbr.org/2013/01/what-is-entrepreneurship.

Ferriss, Timothy. *The 4-Hour Workweek: Escape the 9-5, Live Anywhere and Join the New Rich.* New York: Harmony Books, 2005.

*Guidant Financial.* "Current Trends and Statistics for Aspiring Entrepreneurs." 2019 Trends–Aspiring Entrepreneurs. Accessed on June 27, 2021. https://www.guidantfinancial.com/small-business-trends/aspiring-entrepreneur-trends/.

Guillebeau, Chris. *The $100 Startup: Reinvent the Way You Make a Living, Do What You Love, and Create a New Future.* New York: Currency, 2012.

Lim, Amanda. "China Animal Testing: Limitations Remain for Companies Seeking Exemption from Animal Tests." Cosmetics Design-Asia. January 19, 2021. https://www.cosmeticsdesign-asia.com/Article/2020/09/09/China-animal-testing-Limitations-remain-for-companies-seeking-exemption-from-animal-tests.

reNature. "Homepage." Accessed on June 27, 2021. https://www.renature.co/.

Thought For Food. "Homepage." Accessed on June 27, 2021. https://thoughtforfood.org/

## CHAPTER 6

Borrud, Gabriel and Neil King. "After Coronavirus: Our Relationship with Meat and the Next Pandemic." *DW*, November 20, 2020. https://www.dw.com/en/after-coronavirus-our-relationship-with-meat-and-the-next-pandemic/a-55594449.

Eadicicco, Lisa. "The CEO of Impossible Foods, the Startup behind the Wildly Popular Veggie Burger Backed by Serena Williams and Katy Perry, Shares the Biggest Piece of Advice He Wishes He Knew at Age 20." *Business Insider*, January 16, 2020. https://www.businessinsider.com/impossible-foods-ceo-pat-brown-career-advice-2020-1.

Effective Altruism. "Introduction to Effective Altruism." Accessed on June 27, 2021. https://www.effectivealtruism.org/articles/introduction-to-effective-altruism/.

Feloni, Richard. "How Fear of 'the Biggest Environmental Catastrophe That Our Planet Has Ever Faced' Drove the Founder of $2 Billion Impossible Foods to Go Global." *Business Insider*, May 16, 2019. https://www.businessinsider.com/impossible-foods-ceo-meatless-burger-climate-change-2019-5.

Fortuna, Carolyn. "72% of Impossible Burger Sales Displace Animal-Derived Foods." *Clean Technica*, September 20, 2020. https://cleantechnica.com/2020/09/20/impossible-burger-sales-replace-72-of-traditional-burger-sales/.

Give Well. "Homepage." Accessed on June 27, 2021. https://www.givewell.org/.

Giving What We Can. "Homepage." Accessed on June 27, 2021. https://www.givingwhatwecan.org/.

Green Monday Group. "Group Structure." Green Monday. Accessed on June 27, 2021. https://greenmonday.org/en/group-structure/.

Hansen, James and Fred Gale. "China in the Next Decade: Rising Meat Demand and Growing Imports of Feed." *USDA Economic Research Service*, April 7, 2014. https://www.ers.usda.gov/amber-waves/2014/april/china-in-the-next-decade-rising-meat-demand-and-growing-imports-of-feed/.

Niller, Eric. "An AI Epidemiologist Sent the First Warnings of the Wuhan Virus." *Wired*, January 25, 2020. https://www.wired.com/story/ai-epidemiologist-wuhan-public-health-warnings/.

Poinski, Megan. "Impossible Foods Recruits Scientists to Double R&D Department in 12 Months." *Food Dive,* October 21, 2020. https://www.fooddive.com/news/impossible-foods-recruits-scientists-to-double-rd-department-in-12-months/587398/.

Turner, Laura. "How Eating Less Meat Can Reduce Poverty." *The Borgen Project,* August 12, 2018. https://borgenproject.org/eating-less-meat-can-reduce-poverty/.

Weathers, Scott and Sophie Hermanns. "Open Letter Urges Who to Take Action on Industrial Animal Farming." *The Lancet—Correspondence.* Volume 389, Issue 10084, E9, May 22, 2017. https://www.thelancet.com/journals/lancet/article/PIIS0140-6736(17)31358-2/fulltext.

Williamson, Ben. "Fast Food's Love of Plant-Based Meat Saves a Quarter Million Animals per Year." *World Animal Protection* (blog), December 11, 2019. https://www.worldanimalprotection.us/blogs/fast-foods-love-plant-based-meat-saves-quarter-million-animals-year.

## CHAPTER 7

CISION. "Israel's Prime Minister Tastes Aleph Farms Cultivated Steak." *PRNewswire*, December 7, 2020. https://www.prnewswire.com/il/news-releases/israels-prime-minister-tastes-aleph-farms-cultivated-steak-301187468.html.

Clendaniel, Morgan. "World Changing Ideas 2019: All the Winners, Finalists, And Honorable Mentions." *Fast Company*, April 8, 2019. https://www.fastcompany.com/90329244/world-changing-ideas-2019-all-the-winners-finalists-and-honorable-mentions.

Gunther, Marc. "The Patagonia Adventure: Yvon Chouinard's Stubborn Desire to Redefine Business." *B The Change* (blog), Sep 6, 2016. https://bthechange.com/the-patagonia-adventure-yvon-chouinards-stubborn-desire-to-redefine-business-f60f7ab8dd60.

Harn, Darby. "10 Ways Spider-Man's Relationship with Iron Man Is Completely Different in the Comics." *CBR*, November 18, 2020. https://www.cbr.com/spider-man-iron-man-comics-relationship-differences/.

Keerie, Maia. "Record $3.1 Billion Invested in Alt Proteins in 2020 Signals Growing Market Momentum for Sustainable Proteins." *The Good Food Institute* (blog), March 18, 2021. https://gfi.org/blog/2020-state-of-the-industry-highlights/.

Kenner, Robert, Dir. *Food, Inc.* Los Angeles, CA: Magnolia Home Entertainment, 2009. DVD video.

Russo, Joe, and Anthony Russo, Dir. *Avengers: Infinity War.* Burbank, California: Marvel Studios, Burbank, CA: Buena Vista Home Entertainment, 2018. DVD video.


## CHAPTER 8

*BBC News.* "Hong Kong Protest: 'Nearly Two Million' Join Demonstration." June 17, 2019. https://www.bbc.com/news/world-asia-china-48656471.

Hadano, Tsukasa. "China's Christians Keep the Faith, Rattling the Country's Leaders." *Nikkei Asia*, September 10, 2019. https://asia.nikkei.com/Politics/China-s-Christians-keep-the-faith-rattling-the-country-s-leaders.

Hernández, Javier C. "Harsh Penalties, Vaguely Defined Crimes: Hong Kong's Security Law Explained." *The New York Times*, June 30, 2020. https://www.nytimes.com/2020/06/30/world/asia/hong-kong-security-law-explain.html.

Hui, Mary. "Armed Thugs Returned to the Streets of Hong Kong to Attack Protesters." *Quartz*, August 6, 2019. https://qz.com/1681557/armed-thugs-in-white-attack-protesters-in-hong-kong/.

Hui, Mary. "In Hong Kong, Almost Everyone, Everywhere—Including Pets—Is Getting Tear Gassed." *Quartz*, August 8, 2019. https://qz.com/1683024/police-have-fired-a-record-amount-of-tear-gas-in-hong-kong/.

Hui, Mary and Isabella Steger. "Photos: Hong Kong Police Fight Protesters in a Luxury Shopping Mall." *Quartz*, July 15, 2019.

https://qz.com/1665776/hong-kong-police-clash-with-protesters-in-shopping-mall/.

Parkin, Siodhbhra. "How China Regulates Foreign Non-Governmental Organizations." *The China NGO Project*, August 27, 2019. https://www.chinafile.com/ngo/latest/how-china-regulates-foreign-non-governmental-organizations.

Sala, Ilaria Maria. "Hong Kong is Having Flashbacks to the Bad Old Days of Police Corruption and Mafia Ties." *Quartz*, September 2, 2019. https://qz.com/1695597/hong-kong-police-beat-crouching-protesters-in-subway-train/.

Watts, Alan. *The Way of Zen*. New York: Pantheon Books, 1951.

Wong, Brian and John Mak. "'One Country, Two Systems' Is Still the Best Model for Hong Kong, But It Badly Needs Reform." *Time*, October 30, 2019. https://time.com/5713715/hong-kong-one-country-two-systems-failure/.

## CHAPTER 9

Angry Birds. "Homepage." Rovio Entertainment Corporation. Accessed on June 27, 2021. https://www.angrybirds.com/.

Sekerbayeva, Zhanar. "My Activism Isn't Motivated by Kindness. It's Motivated by Anger." *Amnesty International*, July 2, 2019. https://www.amnesty.org/en/latest/campaigns/2019/07/zhanar-sekerbayeva-from-feminita-on-why-anger-motivates-her-activism/.

## CHAPTER 10

Beyer, Catherine. "Magnum Opus: the Great Work." *Learning Religion*, updated on July 24, 2018. https://www.learnreligions.com/the-great-work-or-magnum-opus-95943.

Fritz, Robert. *Path of Least Resistance: Learning to Become the Creative Force in Your Own Life.* New York: Ballantine Books, 1989.

Kingsnorth, Paul. "The Great Work—Alchemy and the Power of Words." *Emergence Magazine,* October 1, 2018. https://emergencemagazine.org/essay/the-great-work/.

Poushter, Jacob and Nicholas Kent. "The Global Divide on Homosexuality Persists. But Increasing Acceptance in Many Countries over past Two Decades." *Pew Research Centre*, June 25, 2020. https://www.pewresearch.org/global/2020/06/25/global-divide-on-homosexuality-persists/.

The Good Food Institute. *2017 Year in Review.* Washington, DC: GFI, 2018. https://gfi.org/resource/year-in-review-2017/.

Tolle, Eckhart. *The Power of Now: A Guide to Spiritual Enlightenment.* Novato: New World Library, 2004.

## EPILOGUE

*Lifewater* (blog). "World Water Day 2021: 10 Facts About the Water Crisis." February 10, 2021. Accessed on June 27, 2021. https://lifewater.org/blog/world-water-day-2021/.

Lonely Planet. "Tulum." Accessed on June 27, 2021. https://www.lonelyplanet.com/mexico/yucatan-peninsula/tulum.

Zacharias, Nil. "#82—Tashi Nyima: A Buddhist Monk's Perspective on How to Transform the Food Industry and Change the World." April 10, 2019. In *Eat For The Planet*. Produced by Nil Zacharias. Podcast, MP3 audio, 1:20:00. https://eftp.co/tashi-nyima.